The **WRITER'S DIGEST SOURCEBOOK** for

Building Believable Characters

Marc McCutcheon

WRITER'S DIGEST BOOKS
Cincinnati, Ohio

This hardcover edition of *The Writer's Digest Sourcebook for Building Believable Characters* features a "self-jacket" that eliminates the need for a separate dust jacket. It provides sturdy protection for your book while it saves paper, trees and energy.

Other fine Writer's Digest Books are available from your local bookstore or direct from the publisher.

02 01 00 99 98   8 7 6 5 4

Library of Congress Cataloging-in-Publication Data

McCutcheon, Marc.
    The Writer's digest sourcebook for building believable characters / by Marc McCutcheon.
      p.   cm.
    ISBN 0-89879-683-0 (pob. : alk. paper)
    1. Fiction—Technique. 2. Characters and characteristics in literature. I. Title.
PN3383.C4M43 1996
808.3—dc20
                                      95-23746
                                         CIP

Edited by Jack Heffron and Roseann Biederman
Interior and cover designed by Angela Lennert Wilcox
Cover illustration by Peter Fasolino

Speaking of characters . . . to Kara, Macky and Deanna

About the Author

Marc McCutcheon is a writer and lexicographer who lives in South Portland, Maine with his wife, Deanna, and two children, Kara and Matthew.

His most recent books include *Roget's Superthesaurus*, *Descriptionary*, *Writer's Guide to Everyday Life in the 1800s*, and *The Compass in Your Nose & Other Astonishing Facts About Humans*.

Contents

Introduction

If you're like most writers, you probably use your thesaurus on a weekly, if not a daily, basis. The thesaurus is a great memory aid, and it frequently shows us words we might not think of ourselves. Mostly, of course, it prevents us from being too repetitive.

The thesaurus is, indeed, a valuable tool, but if you're like me, you may have—at least on a few occasions—wanted something more from it. For example, when writing fiction, and describing a female character's clothes, I often find myself becoming *tongue-tied*. (Or is that *type*-tied?) Hmmm, what kind of dress *is* that character wearing anyway?

If I turn to my traditional thesaurus, I won't find the answer. Nor will a dictionary help, because I don't know what word to look for in the first place. I have, really, just two choices. I can go to the library and get a book on women's dresses, and therefore burn up a lot of valuable writing time. Or I can take the lazy way out and simply describe the outfit as a "blue dress." I know I can get away with such lameness every now and then. The key is to not let such laxness accumulate.

The trouble is, I have this nomenclature problem not only with women's clothing, but with hats as well. I've never been a good describer of hats. Come to think of it, hairstyles give me trouble, too. If it's not a buzz cut or a ponytail, I simply don't know *what* it is! And with the human face capable of making hundreds of different expressions, why do I always get stuck on using the same tired two, frown and smile, over and over again? Is it because I don't know what to call those other expressions? And what about noses? And subtle tones of voice? And foreign names? And . . . my goodness, is there a book idea here?

Talking to other writers, I learn that the problem can be semi-solved by creating "swipe sheets" or "cheat sheets"; that is, lists of descriptive words and phrases borrowed from other novels or, sometimes in the case of women's dresses, the Sears catalog. One writer has an "ugly noses" file with the word *bulbous* at the top. Over the years, he encountered *gourdlike* and *like an Idaho potato*, all nice schnozzes for a witch, and promptly added them to the file. So when the time came when he needed a really ugly snoot, he didn't settle for *The witch had an ugly nose.* He simply turned to his homemade lexicon for something truly grotesque.

When I discovered how many writers do this sort of thing, something clicked.

Yeah, there was a book idea here, all right. And, necessity being the mother of invention and all that . . .

We bring you the *Writer's Digest Sourcebook for Building Believable Characters.*

This book is not a giant swipe sheet. It's a bona fide thesaurus, designed to be used guilt-free. After all, if you're allowed to look up a *synonym* for nose, why can't you look up a nose *type*? Like the traditional thesaurus, this sourcebook is nothing more than a memory enhancer; a lexicon to jog your imagination and show you words you might not think of (or at least not think of quickly) on your own.

Within these pages, you'll find some 23 different mustaches, 31 noses, 41 beards, 68 shoes and boots, 71 hats, 102 facial types, 117 dresses and skirts, 181 hairstyles, 270 eye types and colors, 360 facial expressions, 5,000 foreign given names and surnames, and thousands of other words and phrases to help you accurately describe your characters from head to toe and from inside out. Personality traits. Quirks. Bad habits. Occupations. Psychological problems. Diseases. And the list goes on and on. Everything you can imagine that goes into the construction of a living, breathing, three-dimensional being that readers can relate to, love, hate, love to hate or hate to love.

Plus, you get advice from six popular novelists on how to put it all together. The how, who, what, where and why from the professionals who have succeeded through trial and error and who can show you how to resuscitate paper-doll characters who refuse to breathe.

Use this sourcebook *before* you begin to write your story. Start with a rough character idea and build point by point, physically, intellectually, psychologically. Write a character profile, a dossier, a history or a secret FBI file. Whatever works. Whatever helps you to visualize the character clearly. But fill it with detail. And remember this advice: If the character is foggy to you, it will be foggy to the reader. Make those details real. Use your imagination. Use your memory. Use your experiences. And use the *Sourcebook for Building Believable Characters.* Try it between your dictionary and your Roget's. We think it'll make a nice fit.

Part One

Creating Great Characters

*M*ost writing how-to books give the opinions of only one writer. We polled *six* popular authors and asked them in detail how they breathed life into their characters. Their answers, although not always in agreement (and there lies the value of having six viewpoints instead of one), provide a primer on how to create three-dimensional characters. Their advice, along with the thesaurus component of this book, will help you create fictional people faster and more realistically than ever before. Study the tips carefully, then refer to the thesaurus component whenever you need help in creating or describing a character's personality and features.

The contributors include:

Sue Harrison. After collecting seventeen rejections, she sold the first novel she ever wrote, a powerful prehistoric saga called *Mother Earth, Father Sky*, to Doubleday in 1990 for a $406,000 advance. The book was a critical and popular success and was soon followed by the second book in the series, *My Sister the Moon*. Harrison lives in Michigan.

Christina Skye. Her first novel, *Defiant Captive* (Dell), won the B. Dalton award for bestselling romance of 1990 and a Romantic Times Reviewer's Choice Award for special achievement. Two bestsellers, *The Black Rose* and *The Ruby*, have followed, with more books planned. "An outstanding new author destined to be one of the stars of the decade," say industry insiders. Skye currently resides in New York.

Johnny Quarles. Elmer Kelton says Quarles "brings a fresh approach to the classic western," and Quarles' editor, Tom Colgan at Avon, says his lightning rise to popularity is "extremely unusual" for a new author. Sales of his first two westerns, *Brack* and *Varro*, were so strong, in fact, that Avon made his third title, *Outlaws*, their lead fiction release for the summer of 1992. Quarles spent several years in radio as a morning talk show host and sports announcer, and five years in the oil business, before trying his hand at writing. He is one of those rare writers who finishes books in just one draft.

Hank Searls. Favored by critics and readers (he is George Bush's favorite author) for his powerful writing style, Searls has authored some 20 million words of published work. His novel, *Overboard* (*not* to be mistaken for the movie with Goldie Hawn), is one of the most frightening sailing disaster novels ever written. The screenplay for TV, also written by Searls, starred Angie Dickinson and Cliff Robertson. In addition to novelizing the movies *Jaws 2* and *Jaws, the Revenge*, some of Searls' critically acclaimed books include *Kataki*, *Sounding*, *The Crowded Sky*, and a "first-man-on-the-moon" novel, *Pilgrim Project*, which became the movie *Countdown*. From his home in Gig Harbor, Washington, Searls currently runs the Hank Searls Authors' Workshop.

O'Neil DeNoux. A former "Homicide Detective of the Year" for the Jefferson Parish Sheriff's Office in New Orleans, his first novel, *Grim Reaper*, was lauded for its super-realistic depictions of homicide investigation. When it comes to portrayals of cops at work, DeNoux pulls no punches. His cop dialogue is among the grittiest in the business, and many of the incidents he describes—from the seamier side of New Orleans life—are based on his own grisly experiences. Following *Grim Reaper* in his cop series are: *The Big Kiss*, *Blue Orleans* and *Crescent City Kills*, all published by Zebra.

John Ames. Like Sue Harrison, Ames also grew up and went to school in Michigan. He has taught writing at various universities and is currently living in New Orleans. He is the author of three horror novels, *The Force, Spellcaster* and *Death Crystal*, and a six-book Western (*Cheyenne*) series, originating in 1992. Ames's teaching experience shows in the advice he gives; his words are among the most insightful, eloquent and thorough of all.

HOW THE PROS CREATE GREAT CHARACTERS

What sort of planning goes into the creation of your characters? What must you know about them before you can tell their story?

Ames: I suspect that most professional writers can pull stock, minor characters out of their hat. But for me, anyway, developing major characters is a top priority of the planning stage. I know it's a cliché, but fiction is almost always about people, and if you don't have good characters, then you haven't got good fiction.

I agree with the notion that most writers project a little of themselves into every major character. That makes perfect sense, since we need something to start with. But I don't carry this too far—it's much easier to make something up than to try to accurately convey autobiographical details. Ironically, I find it simpler to project more of my "real life" into female characters, maybe because that eliminates the obvious temptation of turning a male into myself or another man from my real life.

As far as what you must know before you can tell their story, I side with the "as much as possible" school. It's a good idea to keep character notebooks with a section for expanding each major and the major-minors. The bit players, those characters who pop up for convenience here and there, I think should be handled spontaneously. It isn't necessary to background and profile every bellhop and waitress. But get a good handle on your majors: The idea is to have them so clearly fleshed out before you begin that you know intuitively how they would react in any situation.

Of course, you don't give the reader nearly as much information about your characters as you know. Your notebook should list the character's traits, likes and dislikes, overwhelming passions in life, and of course the fatal bete noire which the character must overcome to grow. Create a wardrobe, stock their fridge, place them in specific crisis situations and ask how they react. How is the character's sex life, and why is it that way? What kinds of friends—and enemies—would this character have?

DeNoux: I build a brief biography of each character in my story. I put in all the pertinent details: physical descriptions, psychology, mannerisms, background information, outer and inner motivations. Sometimes I cut out pictures from magazines in order to better visualize my characters, and glue those pictures to the bios.

Searls: You have to know your characters somewhat better than you know yourself. Date of birth, education, physical characteristics—the works. Write family trees. Then file it all away for reference in case you forget a character's age or eye color. Put your characters in conflict in your manuscript and see what they're made of.

Quarles: Sometimes I know a lot about a character before I start writing. In my novel, *Brack*, I felt as if I knew the main character before I wrote the first paragraph. He was basically an uncle of mine . . . toned down. So it all fell easily into place with very little pre-planning.

Other times, I just sort of start out with a character and learn about him as I go. Common sense tells me that a bad guy will have all sorts of bad traits about him. This may sound like a cop-out, but I honestly don't give a whole lot of early thought to character development. Basically, I learn with the reader. Each character gets a general label from me, and I build from there.

Harrison: I try to remember that if the character is foggy to me as a writer, he or she will be foggy to the reader as well. If I'm having trouble with a character not coming to life, I'll stop and do a character sketch.

Although the "friends as characters" question has already been touched on briefly, it deserves further illumination. Do you use composites of people you know as characters?

Ames: Yes, much of the time. I know a woman who can't go to sleep at night without checking underneath the bed; that gave me one trait for a heroine [in his Mardi Gras thriller, *Spellcaster*] who rolls a tennis ball under the bed every night as part of her ongoing struggle with nyctophobia, fear of the night and darkness. I know another woman who has a pet-peeve thing about smearing lipstick on her teeth. I gave that trait to the same heroine. But I avoid trying to "borrow" a real person's entire personality.

DeNoux: Most of my composites are friends; some are relatives. They get a kick out of it. As for my villains, I base them on real-life villains, such as Son of Sam or Jack the Ripper, or the killers from my real cases. In all instances, I change them around— change their race, sex, description and the like.

Quarles: I've already mentioned Brack and my uncle . . . Minor characters galore are composites of people around me. Some I know, some I have never spoken to. For instance, I might use a newscaster with small ears and a lisp, or a man in a restaurant who never looks at his wife while they eat. He smiles with his mouth, but never looks at her.

Harrison: In *Mother Earth, Father Sky*, Shuganan is based on many of the characteristics of my paternal grandfather.

Searls: After our divorce, my first wife ended up complaining that I used her in my second novel. She was right.

In Ecclesiastes in the Bible is a wonderful quote about names: "Every man has three: one his father and mother gave him, one others call him, and one he acquires himself." Even more apropos is this quote found in Samuel: "As his name is, so is he."
Which brings us to Bilbo Baggins, Scarlett O'Hara, Atticus Finch, Ravenhurst, Huckleberry Finn and Scrooge. The authors

who created these protagonists obviously put great thought into choosing names. Why? What's the rationale behind some of your own name choices?

Skye: Names are *very* important. Often a character doesn't click for me until the name is right. A name can convey so many subtle connotations. The Chinese say that a person rectifies himself to his name; in other words, he *becomes* his name. I think there's a great deal of truth to that. Dickens was a master at naming characters, of course.

DeNoux: For me, it's a matter of feel: The name either *sounds* right for the character or it doesn't. There are probably some wonderfully sophisticated and heroic people in this world named Herb, but I doubt that I'd use that name for any of my heroes. On the other hand, I can imagine a Hitchcockian situation in which a character named Herb is forced by circumstances to act heroically, and succeeds in doing so.

Quarles: I think you choose names to fit the stories, whether they be humorous, catchy, flowery or dramatic. Mark Twain certainly wanted his characters to be humorous and thusly named. In the case of Huckleberry Finn, there is a funny, good-ole-boy, fishing buddy sound to it. Small town, if you will.

Margaret Mitchell chose Scarlett O'Hara because she was Irish and the name has a southern flair about it. I think you find more raw humor in the South than any other region of the country. Names such as Dixie, Annabelle and Florence conjure up certain thoughts and feelings. Even if I'd never heard the name Scarlett before, I surely would have thought of the South, and that's important.

He had rheumy eyes and dark hollows for cheekbones, and his nose projected from his face like an Idaho potato. Then he flashed that awful corn-kernel grin . . .

Physical features. Many authors introduce their characters by describing them from head to toe; others spend little or no time on physical aspects. Do you think physical descriptions are im-

portant? What devices do you find most effective when trying to help a reader visualize a protagonist?

DeNoux: Yes, physical descriptions are important, especially if you give your characters a memorable trait that you can keep showing the reader. James Lee Burke, author of the Dave Robicheux series of crime novels (including Edgar winner *Black Cherry Blues*) is a master of centering on physical traits to reveal character. Elmore Leonard does this quite often with his unforgettable crooks and cops.

I've used the same method. I described my villain in *The Big Kiss* as having a pock-marked face. His nickname was Pus Face. It was successful in turning many a stomach. OK, so that was real obvious, but it worked. I did the same thing in *Blue Orleans*, giving one character pigeon-shit-blue eyes.

Skye: Feed in key details only. Be judicious: It's the telling detail that convinces, not a mound of raw description. Also, find the physical elements that convey interior attitudes, e.g., stiff posture, shifty eyes, thin lips, trembling fingers. I believe the key is the quality of the descriptions, not the quantity.

Quarles: I prefer to describe the person's size more than anything else. Leading characters need to have a sexual image: nice muscles, smooth skin, etc. I don't write romance novels, so I describe male characters as believable in the physical sense—no Prince Valiants. A male character might be described as having huge forearms; when he breaks a man's jaw in a fight in chapter thirteen, you're not surprised, since you've read about his powerful arms in chapter two.

Ames: It's often better to do physical descriptions indirectly, through suggestion. The problem with creating a complete photo of your character is that we all have varying standards of beauty, different traits in the opposite sex that turn us on. Make your heroine too clear for me, and I just might not like her. But give me just enough to shape my ideal, and we're in business.

This gets tricky and poses one of the toughest challenges for all writers. One valuable device I use is what I call "other-reflector characterization." Instead of the author's voice conveying descriptions, other characters do. "Hon, I swear if I had your looks, I wouldn't be paying income tax," my heroine's buddy, an older woman, remarks to her early on; and this follows a scene where my heroine—a bit self-conscious about her sexy new haircut anyway—happens on to a construction scene and the crew goes nuts over her. Readers get the point without my having to go into clichéd raptures about her.

QUICK TIPS ON IMPROVING CHARACTER DESCRIPTIONS

1. Whenever possible, combine a physical description with some form of action. "Sometimes," says Quarles, "if the character has a mustache, I'll have him stroke it thoughtfully. If a woman has blue eyes, I'll have her cast a 'blue-eyed glance' at the hero. An 'active' description gives the reader a motion picture to look at. An 'inactive' one gives only a still-life painting."

Inactive: The woman had a slim frame.

Active: The woman's slim frame shook with laughter as she bent down and tossed an oilskin bag of tea over her shoulder. (Christina Skye, *The Black Rose*)

Inactive: He had rotten teeth.

Active: Inside, he looked toward the bed, then turned his head to grin at the other two, showing a mouthful of broken, rotting teeth. (Johnny Quarles, *Varro*)

2. Be specific, not general. Specific words and phrases give the reader a sharply defined picture; general words give the reader a vague picture.

General: The old witch had an ugly nose.

Specific: The old witch had a nose like a gourd.

The old witch had a bulbous nose.

Combined with an "active" description: The old witch peered down her gourdlike nose and cackled at us.

3. Avoid weighing down descriptions with too many adjectives. Think noun and verb foremost, adjectives second.

Adjective overload: She had beautiful, sensual, ruby red, Cupid's bow lips that men found irresistible.

Less is more: She ran her tongue over moist, Cupid's bow lips.

4. When appropriate, try to reveal some form of emotion behind your description. The goal is to stimulate the reader in as many ways as possible.

Emotionless: Both men were squat and muscular and carried long blowguns.

Emotional: Both men were squat and muscular, both carried long and lethal-looking blowguns, and both looked extremely glum—bored or homicidal or maybe both.

Which is more effective, to simply tell a reader about a protagonist's personality traits or to show them in action?

DeNoux: Always show. That's a basic rule of all fiction. Personality traits can be easily revealed in action. A vicious killer reveals his monstrous side after he kills, when he leans over and bites his victim.

Skye: Absolutely better to show them. This lets the reader make the discovery, and the result is far more persuasive than if the writer made a flat statement.

Harrison: To show. It works the same way as life. I am going to learn more about kayaking by doing it than by reading about it. A reader is "doing" with the character in an action scene; the same reader is only reading when it comes to description.

How is it possible to reveal one character's traits through another character's eyes? Can you recall any examples of this technique from your own work?

Harrison: The best thing about revealing one character's traits through another character's eyes rather than through the more impersonal voice of the narrator is that two processes of characterization are occurring. The reader is getting to know the character being described and also the character doing the describing. I'll give an example from *Mother Earth, Father Sky*:

> Blue Shell, Gray Bird's wife, Chagak thought, and then heard the spirit voice of some sea otter say, "She is beautiful, that woman."
>
> Yes, Chagak thought. Anyone would find pleasure in seeing Blue Shell's tiny nose and wide eyes, her small, full lips. Chagak touched her own face and wondered if anyone found pleasure in seeing her.

Skye: Secondary characters are excellent for this. Information conveyed by secondary characters is usually more convincing because we believe what they have to tell us. It is simply more of a convention that secondary characters won't lie to us. Here's a scene from *Defiant Captive* to show what I mean:

> Behind the duke the groom grimaced and tightened his precarious hold upon the strap at the boot. His Grace was in a rare taking tonight and no mistake—not that Jeffers could blame him. She was a devil from hell, that one, and she would drive any man to recklessness.
>
> Still, it was not like the duke to take his anger out on his cattle. Nor on his servants, for that matter, which was one of the reasons Jeffers liked him so well, for all he could be a stern taskmaster.
>
> The road veered sharply east then, and Jeffers gasped as the well-sprung carriage tilted alarmingly. He held his tongue, however. He knew better than to comment when His Grace was in one of his black moods.

What about weaknesses in characters? After all, Dracula was emasculated by a crucifix, Superman by Kryptonite. Achilles had that dratted heel. Is it coincidence that all of the most memorable heroes and anti-heroes suffer from such vulnerabilities?

Ames: There's a law of fantasy and horror fiction that states: The hero must have *just enough* magic to fight back. A completely invulnerable hero would be a dramatic dud because there would be no suspense when he or she was in danger. And main characters should be in danger a lot.

That means that when they are in trouble, they have to fight hard and rely on their brains and have their strengths—and weaknesses—tested to the limits under stress. A character with a vulnerability is a character who has to *show* character to survive, to triumph and overcome.

Searls: To make a character all-powerful is to send the reader to the TV. If a character has no vulnerabilities, why write the book? This includes Superman, whose vulnerability is his naïveté.

Harrison: How boring to read about a perfect person! I'm not perfect and so cannot identify to a great degree with a character who is. It's that identification, that becoming, that draws the reader into the story.

Quarles: If you don't have vulnerabilities, there's no believability. I don't think you can just create something that doesn't have fallibility to some degree. If a character cannot be defeated, then there's no story. I don't know what the figure is on the percentage of people who believe in God. It seems like I recall a survey that said 85 to 90 percent of us believe in some form of God. For that vast majority, we go on the belief that God is the only infallible thing in the universe. Everything else must have a leak somewhere.

So characters definitely should not be perfect or predictable. But just how realistic should they be? For example, do you ever give the "good guy" at least one unlikable trait? Do you ever give the "bad guy" at least one nice or likable trait? That would be realistic, but is such realism necessary in fiction?

DeNoux: I give my heroes at least one unlikable trait to make them imperfect. I rarely give my villains any likable traits. I guess I'm still too much of a cop. Cops don't give a rat's ass if someone was abused as a child and that's why they kill. Cops are only concerned with who, what, where, when and how. Therefore I don't confuse the reader by giving them something to like in my villains.

John Ames and I were once invited to give a talk to a local chapter of the Romance Writers of America. When talking about characters in recent fiction, several of these women swooned and gushed that they would do anything to meet Hannibal Lecter, the villain from *The Silence of the Lambs.* They found the heroine, Clarice Starling, a bore.

Of course, Harris has created a villain to be remembered, a villain all of us crime writers would love to create. He handles Lecter perfectly. I'm not capable of creating such a great character at this point in my career, so I opt for the evil side, and leave the glamour of super intelligence and animal magnetism to my heroes.

Ames: I'm less likely to give my good guys undesirable traits, but yes indeed, I do give my bad guys desirable traits. Even in the world of popular fiction, it is well understood that "good" and "bad" are ambiguous, fluid concepts anyway. The villain of *The Force* is handsome and suave and has a good sense of humor. Women readers have confessed this made him more interesting to them. Reader interest in your characters is a must. Since something like 70 percent of the readers of paperback fiction are women, it's a good idea to create villains/bad guys with that ambiguous sexiness about them. It's interesting that the villain women readers seem least impressed with in my fiction is one who's so psychotic he's totally bad—he's not only evil and crazy, but ugly, slovenly, totally incapable of flirting or even conversing normally. There's just nothing for the reader to relate to, and he remains a creation, not a solid character.

Quarles: It's been pointed out to me that my bad guys all have a few credible saving graces.

Growing up in such a rough environment with all the different ethnic groups, I saw a lot of tough, mean people. As an adolescent, I knew a lot of so-called scrappers. I was one myself. But I don't think I ever met any of these so-called bad guys who weren't likable in some way. Maybe you had to dig a little, but there was always something good in everyone. I've even read or seen on TV where a killer will win the affections of his interviewer. Capote's *In Cold Blood* is a good example. I read the book so many years ago, I don't recall exactly what the author's feelings were toward the two killers. But in the movie, there's a real sense that he felt for their anguishes and fears in life. Not that the movie portrayed them as good guys—quite the opposite—it shows them as brutal men as they slaughtered the Cutler family. I wanted to kick the shit out of both of the bastards. Still, when they were on death row, and during the hangings, I felt sympathy. It pissed me off, but I still felt it. Somehow, some good qualities had been exposed. For instance, right before killing the family, the Robert Blake character showed compassion for the father, who had been tied up and his limbs were cold. He cut the father loose and put a cover over him. He also didn't allow his partner to rape the daughter. He did take the shotgun and blow the daughter away, but you still felt there was a tinge of decency in the man for not allowing her to be raped. Screwy, isn't it?

Searls: "Badness" and "goodness" are relative. If you want to make a truly bad guy sympathetic to a reader, let him beat up a bad guy who is even worse.

"The cardinal rule is to treat one's characters as if they were chessmen, and not try to win the game by altering the rules—for example, by moving the knight as if he were a pawn." What exactly did George Lichtenberg mean by this statement?

Skye: That characters must be true to their own past and their beliefs, not shoved about simply in service of plot.

Quarles: Presumably he means that once you set up a character with certain strengths and certain limitations, you don't suddenly, at the last minute, give him the ability to see through walls.

Searls: He meant that your characters must move the plot, and your plot not move the characters. He was absolutely right, so you'd better pick characters to start with who will make your plot come to the climax you want. Don't pick a 90-pound weakling to save little Nell in the final scene, if she's being kidnapped by an ape.

Are there any other effective methods of characterization you use and would like to share with the beginning writer?

Ames: There's a bag of tricks for effective characterization. The "dossier" approach is used in mysteries and espionage, where a character's resume is laid out right on the page and studied by the reader and another character. Some variation of this—background letters or other documents—can easily be thought up. Giving the character a bad habit he or she is trying to break—smoking, overeating, cutting people off during conversation—can endear and humanize them for readers. Also, it helps to think dramatically, in terms of the stage "lighting up" when two characters play well off each other. This means tension and difference in personality and speech between them. I still read scenes where three or four cops are standing around and you can't tell them apart when they speak. In real life people seldom sound alike, and they certainly shouldn't in fiction.

Harrison: I like to allow most of my description to be seen through a character's eyes. That way description doesn't become boring and the reader is learning something about the character as well as whatever is being described.

Searls: There are three rules: Conflict, conflict, conflict . . .

What about character growth? Must a protagonist change in some way at the end of a story?

Ames: Yes. Aristotle called this the "recognition and reversal" stage of a drama and attributes it to a deep-rooted human need in the audience to see moral progress in life. If all the hero's struggles have merely saved his life, but not improved it, what good were they?

Searls: The protagonist must either change or learn something about himself, or why write the novel? Novels are parables, after all.

DeNoux: A protagonist should change, but it can be subtle. Your main character should learn something from the ordeal. That's a basic rule. No change, why go through the trouble?

Name a few of the most memorable characters you've encountered in other authors' novels. What do you remember most about them? Did you learn anything from the authors' characterization methods?

Ames: Raskalnikov in Doestoevski's *Crime and Punishment.* The man was a neurotic genius who refused to think according to the parameters of normal society. He's far too "literary" to use as a direct influence in my fiction, but the spirit of his constant, tense mental torment can be borrowed in milder form for, say, the character of a thoughtful detective. Or consider Raymond Chandler's hard-boiled hero, Philip Marlowe. Marlowe stays with me so strongly because of his determination to get at the truth when confronted with a variety of clever lies. To survive he must be truly independent, and I take the spirit of this detective and invest it into my own cop heroes. I'm fascinated by women who flirt well, and Henry James's Daisy Miller has always stayed with me as an excellent example of this type of woman. I try to project her spirit into some of my own flirty female characters. Even if we don't borrow specific traits of other writers' characters, we can borrow the spirit and the intensity they achieved and use it as our standard.

Skye: Jane Eyre and Mr. Rochester. The English narrator in Nevil Shute's *A Town Like Alice.* He is absolutely wonderful, and his point of view gives the story poignancy.

Harrison: Othello, Hamlet, Huck Finn, Scarlett, Nicolo, Jane Eyre. They are alive in my memory as much as real people are.

Searls: Alejandro Stern, in Turow's *Presumed Innocent* and again in his *Burden of Proof*, is off-beat and beautifully limned, and very interesting.

DeNoux: Hoke Mosely in Charles Willeford's Miami series. Here is an overweight detective, besieged with personal problems, including an unfriendly set of dentures, who faces danger with an even temper, who is truly kind and yet capable of brutality when needed.

Quarles: Gus in *Lonesome Dove*. I think he embodied a lot of middle-aged men. Sharp-tongued, witty and full of bullshit. When you get around the blue collar men in America, I think you run into an abundance of this combination. He also showed the reader that a fellow can be west-Texas tough, yet well-read and well-versed at the same time. With Gus, you have a certain amount of Saturday morning Roy Rogers do-good, but you also have a guy who gets shitfaced on occasion, gets horny and can have sex with someone other than his wife. He can be vicious to friends and foes alike, either with his sharp tongue or his gun.

Sidney Sheldon once said that a writer must have natural talent to write believable dialogue, the technique simply cannot be learned. Do you think that's true?

Skye: No. It certainly helps to have a keen ear and a talent for finding the perfect word to delineate a character's background and personality, but practice and ruthless editing can produce nearly the same results.

Searls: Some authors have better ears than others. But dialogue can be vastly improved. If I didn't believe this, I wouldn't be doing my author's workshop.

Quarles: I would agree that it is probably a natural talent in most cases, but I also think that, if a person is open-minded enough, it can be learned.

Harrison: No, but I think it is very difficult to learn.

Ames: I say I "tend" to agree, but I would make one condition. I think we can improve, if not learn, by paying attention to good dialogue. We don't all have natural talent to the same extent, and maybe we can augment what we have through study.

What are some of the tricks you use to reveal character through dialogue?

Skye: Show emotion through the words themselves. By that I mean broken sentences, muttering, stammering, etc. This is the way we really talk, not in grammar-perfect English. Also, don't settle for anything less than the right word in dialogue. Connotations can be so different, and the proper choice of vocabulary pegs a character as nothing else can.

Working a character's thoughts into the dialogue can add nice depth and detail. Here's one way I did it in my novella, *Enchantment*:

> Nicholas's hands tightened as he felt the old gnawing sense of powerlessness begin to choke him.
> "Lord Draycott? Are you there?"
> "I'm here inspector."
> "Are you going to answer my question?"
> Draycott's eyes were unreadable. "Just call it an instinct. Trang and I got to know each other pretty well up there in the jungle. I guess it's often that way between captor and captive. And lately I've had the feeling . . ." *That I'm being watched. That I'm walking right on the edge of a precipice.*
> But Nicholas didn't tell Jamieson that. It would only bring another horde of police flocking down to Draycott Abbey, and all he wanted now was to be left alone.

Searls: Put the characters in conflict. In fiction as in life, you learn more about a person in three seconds of stress than in a lifetime of study.

Quarles: Tricks. I have a hard time thinking in that vein. It just comes natural to me to have an arrogant character say boastful things; a fastidious character may constantly comment on another's lack of cleanliness. One thing that I try to do is give a character some identity through his dialogue. In westerns I may have character A using "dern" and character B using "darn." One character may say "Lordy, Lordy" a lot, whereas another, when excited, will say "hot damn!"

Harrison: Catchwords and phrases, certain pauses, emotional responses. Some characters are more volatile than others and there is more emotion behind their words.

Ames: As I mentioned earlier, I like to have two or more characters talk about a third character who isn't present. This is a good way to characterize several players at once. I'm also a fan of idiolect, the distinctive speaking characteristics of each individual. Formality can be suggested, for example, in a character who forms fewer contractions than the other characters do.

What makes dialogue sound forced or phony?

Searls: Butler-maid dialogue is the worst. This is named for the dusting scene in the old three-act plays where the butler and the maid try to fill in background in Act I, before the main characters arrive.

No two characters should ever mention in dialogue anything that both of them know already; when you do this, all the plumbing shows and you lose the reader.

DeNoux: People don't talk in complete sentences. For some ungodly reason, many of my students figure every sentence has to be grammatically correct, so every piece of dialogue is in complete sentences. People speak in sentence fragments, stutter and correct themselves in the middle of sentences, and use slang and clichés.

Also, direct address can be ridiculous:

"Oh, Ted, I want you."
"Oh, Alice, yes."

"Ted, how old are you anyway?"

"Well, I'm fifty-nine, Alice."

"Taxi!"

Ames: Dialogue that "reads" rather than speaks often sounds forced, as do most political or sentimental comments unless they're very subtly done. This is where the trained ear has to be called in to judge; do these lines sound like spoken lines and do they fit the characters speaking them?

Oddly, I've noticed that often dialogue that is too smooth for too long a time begins to sound forced. Of course, novelists, especially commercial ones, can't recreate the conversational puzzles of a Beckett or Pinter play, but characters can and do misspeak, not hear each other, misunderstand, make bad puns that don't make sense and so forth.

Beginning writers, especially, tend to make dialogue sound forced by using it to advance a cause or espouse—via a first person narrator—personal views and values. Some of them have written great first novels doing this, and all writers somehow include their values in their writing. I've had better luck, though, keeping the political touches light and indirect.

What makes dialogue sound flat or just plain boring?

Searls: Long passages of expository dialogue in which a character, in the guise of talking to another character, *tells* the reader background information. This fools the author, and is the easy way, but it never fools the reader, whose nose for tedium is exquisite.

The problem is that dialogue seems so easy to write, compared to narration or exposition, that the untutored author goes on forever, in passage after passage. You should learn to suspect any paragraph of dialogue over three lines long.

Quarles: When a character has no distinguishing traits of his own, then he has no personality, and his dialogue is most likely going to lack magnetism.

If you don't have characters' idiosyncracies appearing in dialogues, they'll sound unnatural. One thing I like to do is mumble to myself when I'm writing dialogue. I've found that if it doesn't roll off my tongue comfortably, then it's not going to read any better. I try to act out the individual part and write the dialogue in the exact way that person would express himself.

DeNoux: Too much exposition and plot explanation is flat and boring. Dialogue that tells you everything can be boring. A writer needs to be selective.

Ames: Giving speeches, and dialogue that hasn't got any point. All dialogue can't be tense, of course, but I try for as much tension as possible.

Writers sometimes use dialogue for the wrong reasons: "Well, here we are at the Batcave, Robin!" Sometimes, instead of using dialogue to give essential but mundane information to the reader, the info should just come in a tight paragraph of good exposition. The dialogue can then be reserved to heighten the dramatic tension of the scene. Let accusations fly, old wounds be licked, grudges be dredged up, and buried emotions come out.

I try to have an ongoing source of tension automatically built into every dialogue between my male and female love interests. This heightens romance and tragedy. In *The Force*, both feel an intense but unspoken guilt because they loved each other and the woman's husband, who died in an "accident" she knows was suicide, knew it. They never consummated that love nor even admitted it to anyone, but it makes them hyperaware of every comment, sensitive to any shade of meaning in the comments of others. In *Death Crystal*, the male hero doesn't realize the heroine is a beating and rape victim and says some insensitive thing about her "penis fear." When he learns the truth from an old news clipping, it charges all their subsequent verbal interactions with subtextual tension.

Do you contrast speaking styles between two or more characters? How is this done?

Quarles: In *Brack*, Hattie likes to use the saying, "Oh, skittle!'', whereas her daughter wouldn't be caught dead making such a comment. In *Lonesome Dove,* Augustus McRae liked to use the term "I God" when he wanted to talk down to someone. I think it's of the utmost importance to contrast speaking styles. That is as important as making the characters look different. Using different speaking styles creates tension, conflict, romance, attraction of opposites, humor—any emotion you'd like to drum up. For example, one character might become angry, while the other responds with a humorous comeback. That really eliminates the need to say in narrative that one character is infuriating the other. You can have every character in your book recite the same line, but you have to keep each character's idiosyncracies consistent within his development to give the line the meaning you want to convey.

To contrast styles, just quote the character in the way he would make a statement. It helps, again, to say the quote out loud. A cowboy or itinerant farm worker wouldn't use the same grammar that a business executive or a debutante would. If you bring two such extremes together in the same scene, then both components of the dialogue would have to be very different.

DeNoux: I distinguish between them only if there is a difference in the way they speak. For instance, one of my recurring characters, Paul Snowood, uses a country accent. He works at it and tries to sound more country than he is. Therefore, when he's excited, he tends to lose the accent, which is pointed out by other characters.

Ames: Speaking styles will automatically contrast if you are taking care to differentiate each main character. Seldom, if we're really listening, do real people sound alike when they speak. I know a writer isn't doing his or her job when it becomes necessary to have a narrative tag after each utterance so I will know who is speaking. If the writer is doing the job right, we'll usually know who's speaking simply from what's said and how it's said. One character swears easily, another does not; one chooses formal diction with few contractions, another speaks informally with lots of contractions; one character speaks in cryptic grunts, another pontificates. Even if two characters are from the same ethnic and social class—say, two college professors from Boston—they will display unique features of their idiolect, the speaking style specific to an individual.

Are you content to follow a passage of dialogue with "he said/ she said" or do you favor descriptive speech tags, e.g., gasped, muttered, exclaimed, moaned, barked, roared, hissed, purred, etc.?

Searls: Use "said." Nothing is simpler or more professional.

Ames: I'm usually happy with a simple "he said, she said," and I'll even avoid those if they aren't absolutely necessary. The ideal is to have the dialogue so clear through distinct characterizations that narrative tags aren't often needed. However, editors vary on this point. My western editors have instructed me to include plenty of tags so there can not be the slightest doubt as to who is speaking. But they do *not* like too many synonyms for a simple "said." This distracts the reader, again, from the focus on characters and what they're saying. Also, the word "hissed" is used too often, and when it is used it's usually used illogically. Realistically, if the character "hisses" something, it'd better have some sibilant or "s" sounds in it. Where's the logic of " 'Go to hell,' she hissed"?

In general, I tend to avoid descriptive modifiers, which then calls special attention to them when you do carefully select one for effect. If everyone has been gasping and moaning and barking and roaring for fifty pages, it hardly matters if the hero suddenly "shouts" something at the end of the scene. This might become more significant, however, if a simple "said" had set the tone first.

Quarles: I usually just say "said." Sometimes I might use "shouted" or "muttered." The narrative around the quote—and the quote itself—usually pretty much expresses what the character is feeling. I think words like "barked," "hissed" or "purred" are used when the narrative is not descriptive enough or the dialogue is on the shallow side. I think they use these modifiers a lot in romance novels. I'm not putting down romance novels; I've just noticed an abundance of these words in the few I've read.

I'll return to an old standby here, Larry McMurtry. Of all the contemporary writers, his style is most pleasing to me. If you look at *Lonesome Dove*, you'll see that it's full of "he said" and "she said." My thinking is, "Hell, this is a lot easier." It eliminates those long moments spent trying to think of a dynamic verb to use. So far, I have not had one negative comment from my readers on this matter.

Skye: Descriptive verbs other than "said" can be useful as long as they're not overdone. Nothing is more awkward than a page of dialogue dotted by every permutation of the word "said." Often no verbs are necessary at all. I prefer to let the actual dialogue stand on its own.

A snarl of agony crossed the old man's face. Marsha grinned insipidly. Anne set her jaw in mock defiance. Egbert scowled back at her.

The human face is capable of forming hundreds of expressions. How do you describe them all, and can they be used to enrich dialogue or do they detract from it?

Searls: All of these examples are unacceptable. They sound pulp-like and amateurish. They will turn off an agent or an editorial reader instantly. Get rid of the purple adjectives and adverbs. Let the dialogue itself express the mood, by brevity or with expletives or with phrasing, and see how much more professional the dialogue looks.

Speech verbs become redundant if the dialogue is written right. If you correctly write a piece of dialogue, most speech tags and gestural pauses become redundant.

Harrison: Facial expressions are an important part of dialogue, and short descriptions of these expressions can be thrown into a dialogue in that place where, if this were an actual conversation, a natural pause would take place. The reader catches this pause and the conversation seems more realistic. Facial characteristics also convey the emotions that written words do not.

Skye: Facial expressions can be very compelling, as long as they're not overdone. You don't need to describe every facial gesture, only the key ones. It helps to observe gestures and to remember those that are striking.

Ames: Because the human face can be so expressive and subtle, it adds an entire new dimension of possibility to dialogue. But it shouldn't be overdone. You want the main attention on the dialogue.

Do you ever write a narrative passage only to find that it works better presented as dialogue? Do you ever do the reverse?

Searls: Yes. Any time you can advance the story with a scene of two characters in an argument, you're better off than using narrative or exposition. You're showing, not telling.

The reverse? Sure. Any time you can substitute a short narrative summary for a long passage of expository dialogue or lifeless dialogue between two characters who aren't in conflict, you're better off; long passages of dialogue going nowhere are even more boring than long passages of exposition.

Quarles: There are periods when it seems like I'm caught up in nothing but narrative in telling a story, and this will concern me. Then, one day I sit down to write, and the only thing that will come forth is dialogue. This, likewise, scares the dickens out of me. There's always some little voice talking in my ear, telling me I've lost it—that I don't know what I'm doing. It gets so crazy at times, I'll actually grab another author's book and read parts of it to find out how to mix the two together. But you know what? When it's all said and done, and I'm reading over my work with the dialogue vs. narrative issue out of mind, I don't notice that I'm using either one to extreme over the other. I guess it's all in my head.

Just go with however it flows smoothest and don't look back.

Ames: It's easy to mistakenly cast exposition or narrative as dialogue and vice versa. The key, I think, is tension. If you have a key fact, say, the untimely death of a child, and it lends itself to dramatic tension in the unfolding, why relate it in exposition? There are times when it's better to see a dramatic fact acted out rather than summarized after the fact. There are also times when information conveyed in dialogue would work better as simple narrative: Why have characters waste interaction just to cover, say, necessary travel arrangements? In general, try to reserve dialogue for heightening suspense and tension.

DeNoux: It all has to do with pacing. To keep a consistent pace, you must be able to change things around like that.

Do you recall any novels in which the dialogue made a particularly strong impression on you? Did you learn anything from these novels?

Skye: Jane Austen's works because of their honed wit. Georgette Heyer because of her marvelous use of Regency vernacular. C.S. Forester for the Hornblower books, where we get such a rich sense of naval life conveyed completely through dialogue. Anything by Evelyn Waugh, because he's so clever and slyly wicked.

Harrison: I spent a long time studying Hemingway's work. John Gardner and Mark Twain do a great job on conveying dialect and still maintaining readability. Anne Tyler is excellent at conveying personality through a character's speech patterns.

Searls: Any of Hemingway's works. Dashiell Hammett wrote good dialogue. So did Damon Runyon.

Ames: Watching how Elmore Leonard's characters speak has taught me that simple is best; there should be as little authorial machinery as possible coming between writer and reader. Leonard mixes the authorial voice with the character's voice so subtly that the writer often seems to disappear.

And really, though he's a playwright, Neil Simon's dialogue is well worthy of study by any writer. Like Dean Koontz, he has mastered the art of fast, rat-a-tat-tat dialogue that bounces along with minimal intrusion from the writer, yet stays distinct in the reader's mind.

DeNoux: Probably Elmore Leonard. He uses it simply and captures the true sound of people's voices. He doesn't use dialogue to explain things.

Quarles: I don't know if you'd call it dialogue, but the letters in *The Color Purple* were unique. The book made a lasting impression on me. That's the only book, aside from *Lonesome Dove*, that really made an impression. An Elmore Leonard novel has memorable dialogue, too.

Part Two

Character
Questionnaire

CHARACTER QUESTIONNAIRE

Fill out this section thoroughly before starting your story. It will help you focus on who your character is and suggest ways to breathe life into him or her for your readers. Refer to the thesaurus section for help in areas like "body type," "hair styles" and so forth.

Name:

Age:

Height:

Weight:

Body Type:

Physical Condition (Fit, unfit or something in between?):

Eye Color:

Hair Color and Style:

Distinguishing Features:

1.

2.

3.

Physical Imperfections/Would Like Most to Change:

1.

2.

3.

Characteristic Gestures:

1.

2.

Race:

Ethnic Group:

Religion:

Family Background/Lineage:

Years of Schooling:

Major and Minor Studies in College:

1.

2.

3.

Degrees:

Grades Achieved in School:

Special Occupational Training:

Skills, Abilities and Talents:

1.

2.

3.

4.

Areas of Expertise:

1.

2.

3.

Occupation:

Past Occupations:

1.

2.

3.

Military Experience:

Short-Term Goals:

1.

2.

3.

Long-Term Goals:

1.

2.

3.

Short-Term Needs:

1.

2.

3.

Long-Term Needs:

1.

2.

3.

General Personality Type (See Personality Traits Inventory

for help):

Introvert/Extrovert:

Quirks:

1.

2.

3.

Eccentricities:

1.

2.

3.

IQ:

Temperament:

Method of Handling Anger or Rage (Repress, throw things,

etc.):

Admirable Traits:

1.

2.

3.

4.

Negative Traits:

1.

2.

3.

4.

Bad Habits/Vices:

1.

2.

3.

4.

Prejudices:

1.

2.

3.

Pet Peeves and Gripes:

1.

2.

3.

Things That Make Uncomfortable or Embarrass:

1.

2.

3.

Most Painful Things in One's Life:

1.

2.

3.

Ever Been Arrested? (If so, for what?):

1.

2.

3.

Political or Social Issues Most Important To You:

1.

2.

3.

4.

Opinion on Abortion:

Opinion on Environmental Issues:

Opinion on Homosexuality:

Opinion on Military Intervention:

Opinion on Progress:

Opinion on Crime and Gun Control:

Opinions Peculiar to Character:

Political Party:

Liberal, Conservative, Middle of the Road, Radical:

Income:

Sense of Humor (None, dry, understated, witty, slapstick,

   dirty, etc.):

Fears:

1.

2.

3.

Phobias:

1.

2.

3.

Manias:

1.

2.

3.

Physical Illnesses or Afflictions:

1.

2.

3.

4.

Mental Disturbances:

1.

2.

3.

Hobbies:

1.

2.

3.

Interests:

1.

2.

3.

Sports:

1.

2.

3.

Favorite Pastime:

Favorite TV Shows:

1.

2.

3.

Favorite Movies:

1.

2.

3.

Favorite Travel Destination:

Pets:

Drinks Alcohol? (How often?):

Favorite Alcoholic Drink:

Favorite Meal:

Favorite Books:

1.

2.

3.

Diet (Rich, low-fat, low cholesterol, restaurant, etc.):

Favorite Restaurant/Ethnic Food:

Favorite Physical Attributes in Opposite Sex:

Attributes About Character That Turn On Opposite Sex:

Sexual Turn-Ons:

1.

2.

3.

Sexual Turn-Offs:

1.

2.

3.

Traumas/Psychological Scars from the Past:

1.

2.

3.

Clothing Styles/Favorite Outfit:

Favorite Pet Sayings, Words/Idiolect:

1.

2.

3.

Speaking Style (Talkative, taciturn, soft-spoken, loud, formal, casual, accent, fast, slow, etc.):

Philosophy of Life:

Type and Number of Close Friends:

Best Friend:

Other Friends:

Most Crucial Experience (Or experiences that helped to mold

character's personality or attitude):

Home (Apartment/tenement building/high-rent/low-rent dis-

trict/house/mansion/castle, etc.):

Neighborhood:

Car:

Color:

Drive Fast or Slow/Obey Traffic Laws:

Major Problems to Solve or Overcome:

1.

2.

3.

Solutions to Problems:

1.

2.

3.

Minor Problems to Solve or Overcome:

1.

2.

3.

Solutions to Problems:

1.

2.

3.

4.

5.

6.

Character Growth (by the end of the story)/Character Change/

Lessons Learned:

Chronology of Actions (From start of story to end):

1.

2.

3.

4.

5.

6.

7.

8.

9.

10.

11.

12.

13.

14.

15.

16.

17.

18.

Part Three

Character
Thesaurus

1

Face and Body

COMPLEXIONS AND SKIN TYPES

acned: pimples, pustules, or cysts brought on by hormonal changes.

alabaster: pale yellowish-pink to yellowish-gray.

albino: lacking in skin pigmentation. Also known as achromasia.

alligator: a descriptive term for rough, coarse or scaly skin.

apple blossom: silky white.

apple-cheeked: red cheeks.

black: pitch black.

blanched: white or pale, as if bleached out, occurring naturally or as a result of fear or trauma.

blemished: pimples, pustules, cysts, blebs, moles, warts, blackheads, etc.

blue-black: a variation of black.

blush: rosiness or redness, as from embarrassment.

bronze: reddish-brown.

brown: color.

burlap: rough, coarse; also, the color of burlap.

cadaverous: corpse-like; leaden, cyanotic or colorless.

café au lait: the color of coffee with cream.

café noir: the color of black coffee.

caramel: light or medium brown.

chalky: white, gray or yellowish; the color of someone who is sick or deathly ill.

charcoal: dark gray.

chestnut: rich brown.

China doll: white.

China silk: silky.

cinnamon: yellowish-brown.

coal: black.

cocoa: brown.

cratered: pitted or rough from acne or chicken pox.

cream: creamy white.

crimson: deep red.

cyanotic: blue or bluish tinge caused by lack of oxygen in the blood.

doughy: the color of bread dough, or resembling the consistency of it.

downy: very soft and smooth.

ebony: dark or black.

eggshell: white or light brown.

fair: light-colored and unblemished.

florid: flushed red, pink or rosy.

flush: to become red in the face; blush.

freckled: ginger speckles or spots.

ginger: sandy or reddish-brown.

glowing: flushed; healthy.

golden: yellowish or yellow-brown.

greasy: oily.

hay: golden brown or tan.

honey: golden brown or silky-smooth.

humus: the color of rich, black soil.

ivory: creamy white.

jaundiced: a yellowish complexion (it also affects the eyeballs) caused by hepatitis or other medical condition.

leaden: the color of lead. Someone who is very sick or suffering from a heart attack may be described as having a leaden complexion.

leathery: a tough, brown, hide-like skin, as a farmer might have from years of sun exposure.

lentil: light or medium brown.

lily-white: white.

livid: grayish-blue or lead-colored, or black and blue, as a bruise. Corpses are livid in color due to pooled, oxygen-depleted blood.

lobster: severely sunburned.

magnolia: white or pink.

midnight: dark or black.

milky: white or smooth.

molasses: brown.

moled: having moles.

mottled: blotchy.

nubby: rough.

nut-brown: broad variability, from light to dark brown.

ocher: dark yellow or reddish-brown.

olive: dark brown or black.

pale: blanched, white.

pallid: pale, faint or wan.

pasty: like paste in color or texture.

peach: orange-yellow.

pink: color.

pitch: black.

pitted: from acne, chicken pox, etc.

pizza-faced: slang term for one with severe acne.

pocked: cratered, pitted skin, from acne, chicken pox, etc.

pustuled: acned.

razor-burned: red, irritated skin from shaving.

red as a cardinal: descriptive red.

rosy: descriptive red.

ruddy: healthy red.

russet: yellowish-brown or reddish-brown.

rust: orange, reddish-brown or reddish-yellow.

saffron: orange-yellow.

sallow: sickly yellow or pale yellow.

sandalwood: light brown.

sandpaper: rough, coarse.

scarlet: very bright red.

scarred: cut, marred, disfigured.

scrubbed: fresh-faced, or red from scrubbing too hard.

sepia: dark reddish-brown.

sole of an old army boot: descriptive line for rough, as-though-treaded-on, skin.

splotchy: irregular, blotchy.

strawberries and cream: creamy, with red cheeks.

sun-browned: suntanned.

sunburned: red.

swarthy: a dark complexion.

tar: black.

teakwood: yellowish-brown.

wan: pale.

warty: having warts.

waxy: pasty, cadaverous, greasy or oily.

weatherbeaten: weathered by years in the sun; leathery or lined like an old boot.

wheat: tannish or brown.

withered: dried up, weathered, shriveled; without vigor or freshness.

wizened: same as withered.

BLEMISHES

age spots: brown spots on the face and hands, occurring in the elderly. Also known as liver spots.

chloasma: also known as the "mask of pregnancy," brown patches that frequently appear on the skin of pregnant women. It sometimes forms a simple, false mustache over the upper lip.

dermatitis: any inflamed skin.

eczema: skin inflammation characterized by redness, crusting, and the formation of pimples and vesicles.

lentigo: a brownish spot unrelated to a freckle.

liver spots: yellowish-brown, red or black spots or patches on the skin, often appearing in the elderly and formerly attributed to liver disfunction. Also known as age spots.

lupus erythematosus: a skin disease characterized by a scaly rash, often a butterfly pattern over the nose and cheeks.

nevus: any birthmark.

piebald skin: a mysterious skin condition characterized by patches of skin lacking pigment. Also known as vitiligo.

port wine stain: a wine-colored birthmark, as on the forehead of former Soviet leader Mikhail Gorbachev.

rosacea: an inflammatory skin disorder characterized by small pimples and the dilation of facial capillaries, giving a raw, red appearance; often found on the nose and sometimes on other parts of the face. The disorder is common among people originating from the British Isles, alcoholics, and people who blush easily.

strawberry birthmark: a common birthmark, reminiscent of a strawberry.

zits: slang for pimples, acne.

EYE TYPE AND SHAPE

almond: almond-shaped.

banjo: wide, circular eyes.

beady: small and round.

bug: protruding.

bulging: See exophthalmic.

bullish: a descriptive term; fierce.

button: small and round or large and round.

close-set: eyes that are set close together but not quite crossed.

crescent: half-moon shaped, either naturally or when grinning. *Her eyes were mirthful crescents.*

cross-eyed: See strabismus.

cue ball: very large, bulging eyes. See exophthalmic.

deep-set: set deeply into the skull, most pronounced with a prominent forehead ridge.

dewdrop: the shape of a teardrop.

egg-shaped: large ovoid.

esotropic: a form of strabismus in which one eye is turned or crossed inward toward the nose.

exophthalmic: eyes that bulge from their sockets, usually due to a thyroid condition.

exotropic: a form of strabismus in which one eye is turned or crossed outward, away from the nose.

falcon: a descriptive term; a small, round dark eye; bird-like.

feline: cat-like, with lentil-shaped pupils.

fish: glassy and emotionless.

gimlet: piercing; penetrating.

glassy: dull.

goggle: prominent or bulging; also rolling eyes.

hollowed eye sockets: a descriptive term for deep-set eyes, most likely to appear in people who are anorexic or malnourished.

hooded: lids covering part or half of the eyes; sleepy-eyed or bored eyes.

kidney-shaped: reniform, occurring naturally when smiling.

lentil, lenticular: shaped like a lentil or bioconvex lens; the most common eye shape.

luminous: a descriptive term for an animal's eye when reflecting light at night. The reflective eye layer itself is called the *tapetum*.

lunulate: crescent-shaped.

owlish: wide, round and alert.

pea: tiny and round.

pop: protuberant or bulging.

puffin-like: in the shape of a teardrop.

rheumy: watery, moist.

saucer: large or goggle-like. *She regarded the snake with saucer-like eyes.*

shark-like: cold and indifferent.

slits: narrow.

sloe: large and dark, or almond-shaped.

spaniel: round and moist.

squinty: near-sighted or far-sighted.

strabismus: the condition of squinting.

sunken: deep eye sockets, an effect that accompanies anorexia or malnourishment.

walleyed: large, glossy eyes. Also, an eye that turns outward, or a whitish or light-colored iris.

wide-set: set far apart under the forehead.

EYE COLORS

Brown

acorn: weathered nut-brown.

autumn leaf: reddish-brown to brown.

biscuit: light toasted brown.

bronze: reddish-brown or coppery brown.

burnt almond: dark brown.

camel: medium brown.

Congo: muddy or dark brown, after the African river (renamed Zaire River in 1971).

dun: dull grayish-brown.

dusky: dark, shadowy, as in deepening twilight.

dusty road: light brown if dry, dark brown after a rain shower.

earth: broad variability, the entire spectrum of brown.

ebony: very dark brown or black.

elk: medium to dark brown.

fawn: pale, yellowish-brown.

fox: reddish-brown.

Grand Canyon: broad variability, from light to dark browns to reddish-browns.

grizzly bear: variable; brownish, grayish or yellowish.

gunmetal: black.

hawk brown: yellowish-brown, medium brown or grayish-brown.

hazel: reddish-brown or yellowish-brown, usually flecked with green or gray.

honey: yellowish-brown or golden brown.

humus: rich soil brown; dark brown or black.

kelp: seaweed brown.

leather: medium to dark brown; reddish-brown.

lentil: light to medium brown.

lignite: brownish-black.

mahogany: dark reddish-brown or yellowish-brown.

mill pond: deep brown or black.

mink: dark brown.

Mississippi: muddy brown, as found in parts of the river.

moccasin: same as leather.

molasses: usually dark brown.

mottled: flecked, streaked, spotty or blotchy.

mud: broad variability, from light to dark red.

Nubian: medium brown.

nut-brown: broad variability, from yellowish brown to dark brown.

obsidian: very dark or black.

olive: dark brown or black.

otter: medium to dark brown.

raisin: reddish-brown or black.

raven: black.

Rio Grande: muddy.

russet: yellowish- or reddish-brown.

sandy: yellowish, grayish or medium brown.

sienna: yellowish-brown. Burnt sienna is reddish-brown.

soot: grayish-brown or black.

sorrel: light brown or light reddish-brown; dried autumn leaf.

sparrow brown: grayish-brown.

tarnished penny: reddish-brown.
taupe: dark brownish-gray; moleskin.
tawny: brownish-yellow or tan.
umber: the color of shadow.
weathered acorn: medium brown.

Blue, Violet, Gray and Green

apple green: light green.
azure: sky blue.
baby blue: very light to very pale greenish- or purplish-blue.
bittersweet nightshade: purplish-blue, similar to passionflower.
blueberry: light to medium blue.
blue jay: light blue.
bottle green: dark to grayish-green.
celestial blue: sky blue.
cobalt: deep, vivid blue. Also strong greenish-blue.
cornflower: blue or purple.
denim: the color of jeans.
dove gray: grayish-blue or grayish-brown.
electric blue: bright neon blue.
emerald: strong yellowish-green.
gentian: blue.
grape: blue or purple.
holly green: medium to dark green.
hyacinth: deep purplish-blue to vivid violet.
ice: very light blue.
indigo: dark blue to grayish, purplish-blue.
iridescent: having rainbow-like or shifting colors, depending on the angle they're seen from.
iris: light purple.
jade: pale green.

jungle: leaf green.

kingfisher: blue-gray.

lagoon blue: broad variability, from light, crystal blue to dark blue.

lagoon green: broad variability, from light to dark green.

lapis lazuli: sky blue to deep blue.

larkspur: blue to medium purple.

lavender: pale to light purple or very light, very pale violet.

lightning: thunderbolt blue; light, silvery blue.

lilac: pale or light to medium purple.

mauve: brilliant violet or purple, or medium reddish-purple.

midnight blue: very dark blue.

misty blue: very light blue.

morning glory: purplish-blue. Same as passionflower.

moss: medium to dark green.

Nordic blue: light to medium blue.

olive green: light to medium green.

passionflower: purplish-blue.

peacock blue: medium to dark or strong greenish-blue. Also iridescent blue.

pea green: yellowish-green.

periwinkle: purplish-blue.

plum: dark purple to deep reddish-purple.

powder blue: medium to pale blue, or purplish-blue.

Prussian blue: medium to dark blue.

rainforest green: misty leaf green.

royal purple: medium to strong violet, or deep purple.

sapphire: blue.

sea green: broad variability, medium to very dark green.

sea smoke: very light silvery blue or gray.

sky blue: also known as azure.

slate: dark gray to bluish-gray.

smoke: gray-blue.

smoked glass: gray or dark gray.

snow shadow: shadowy blue.

star: twinkling light blue or green.

steel: dark gray to purplish-gray.

storm sea: very dark blue to dark gray.

teal: medium or dark bluish-green to greenish-blue.

terre verte: French term for "green earth"; an olive green.

twilight: dark purple.

violet: reddish-blue to purplish-blue.

Virginia bluebell: blue to purplish-blue.

wild lupine: light to medium blue.

wisteria blue: purplish.

Miscellaneous Eye Variations

bloodshot: red and irritated.

cataract: a clouding of the lens.

glass eye: a false eye of any color.

helerochroma iridis: the condition of having one brown eye and one blue eye. It occurs in approximately 1 in every 1,000 people.

nystagmus: a disorder in which one or both eyes jerk or move involuntarily, caused by brain lesions, inflammation, alcohol or drug abuse; sometimes present congenitally.

variegated: flecked with various colors.

walleyed: having a whitish or grayish eye or eyes.

yellowed scleras: yellowed whites of the eyes, sometimes seen in older people.

NOSES

aquiline: hooked or curved, like an eagle's beak.

bob: knoblike.

boxer's: broken, misshapen.

bulbous: large, shaped like a bulb.

button: round and small.

chiseled: giving the appearance of plastic surgery.

corrected and pampered: formed by a plastic surgeon.

flaring: flaring nostrils.

gourdlike: misshapen, warty or gnarled, like a gourd.

gumdrop: small and dainty.

hawk: aquiline.

hog-nosed: like a pig's snout.

hooked: curved, aquiline.

potato: very large and misshapen, like an Idaho potato.

prissy: high-cut nostrils.

pug: short, flattened and somewhat turned up at the end.

retroussé: turned up at the tip.

rhinophyma: a red and grossly enlarged nose; a disorder of alcoholics and people from the British Isles. Also known as rum nose, rummy nose, toper's nose and whiskey nose.

Roman: having a high, distinctive bridge.

rosacea: a skin condition causing reddening of the nose, most commonly found in alcoholics, people from the British Isles, and people who flush easily.

ruddy: reddish-colored.

skewed: crooked.

snub: short and turned up; pug.

turned-up: retroussé.

whiskey nose: See rhinophyma.

HAIR

Colors

acorn
alabaster
ash
ash blond
auburn
black
bleach blond
blond
blue-gray
bone
brown
brunette
buckskin
burnt almond
café au lait
caramel
carrot
chestnut
chocolate
cinnamon
coal black
cocoa
coffee
copper
dusky

fair-haired
fawn
fiery
flaming
flaxen
flint
fox
golden
gray
grizzled
henna
hoary
honey
ivory
jet-black
lily
magnolia
mahogany
maple sugar
mocha
nut-brown
nutmeg
peroxide blond
platinum blond
polished wood

premature gray
raven
russet
rust
sable
salmon
salt and pepper
sandalwood
sandy
silver
smoke
snowy
straw
strawberry blond
tarnished sunset
tawny
technicolor
  (dyed punk)
titian
tow-headed
vanilla
violent red
washed-out
white

Textures

billowing	flyaway	rigid
bird's nest	frazzled	ropey
bouncy	frizzy	satiny
bristly	fuzzy	shaggy
bushy	greasy	shocked
coarse	kinky	silky
cornsilk	knotted	snarled
crimped	lacquered	spiky
crinkly	listless	stringy (like
dollish	lustrous	twine)
downy	luxurious	thatched
eiderdown	matted	wiry
fine (baby fine)	nappy	wispy
fleecy	oily	woolly
flowing	rat's nest	

Styles

Afro: a kinky, bushy style of the 1960s and early 1970s.

Afro puffs: kinky, bushy puffs worn on either side of the head.

American Indian: long and straight; parted in the middle, braided or worn in a ponytail.

bangs: a fringe of hair falling over the forehead.

Beatle cut: the classic bowl-like cut that reached the height of popularity in the 1960s. Also known as the Moe (Three Stooges) cut.

beaver tail: a flat loop of hair worn over the nape of the neck, originating in 1865. Also known as a banging chignon.

beehive: a very tall, dome-like style reminiscent of a beehive. Popularly worn from the late 1950s to early 1960s.

bob: a woman's or child's short haircut with or without bangs.

bouffant: a full, puffed-out style dependent on copious amounts of hairspray to keep it together.

boyish bob: a woman's very short haircut shingled in the back.

braids: plaited hair. May be worn down the back, to the sides, or wound around the head.

brushed back severely: brushed abruptly away from the face.

bun: a tight roll held fast near the top of the head or near the nape of the neck. Also known as a French roll.

chignon: a knot or roll twisted into a circle or figure eight at the back of the head.

China doll: short and straight with bangs.

Cleopatra: long and straight down the sides.

coiled: a coil of plaits, worn on back, to the side, or on top of the head.

corkscrew curls: long, dangling curls resembling corkscrews.

cornrows: a style in which hair is braided into tight rows close to the head.

crew cut: a flattop or buzz cut, usually only worn by men.

dreadlocks: tight, dangling, shoulder-length braids originally worn by the Rastafarians of Jamaica.

ducktail: a classic 1950s style in which the hair was oiled, combed back over the ears, and molded up in back to form what looked like the tail of a duck. Also known as a DA (duck's ass).

earmuffs: braids worn in circles over the ears.

elflocks: tangled or matted hair.

empire cone: a style, revived by Madonna, in which the hair is pulled through a cone-like contrivance and worn as a ponytail from the top of the head.

fade: also known as the gumby or the slope, a flattop cut at a slant, sometimes with shaved lines or designs through it, a popular style among young men in the 1990s.

feather cut: a woman's layered, slightly curled bob, popular in the 1960s and early 1970s.

fishbone braid: a braid, reminiscent of the spine of a fish, worn down the back. Also known as a French braid.

flattop: crew cut, buzz cut.

flip: a woman's cut in which the hair ends in curls on the sides, usually worn with bangs.

French braid: See fishbone braid.

hardened with hairspray: overly sprayed, giving a brittle or lacquered look.

Mandinko: a look popularized by the television hero, Mr. T., comprised of a Mohawk haircut worn with a beard, mustache and sideburns.

marcel wave: tight waves arranged around the head with a curling iron, originating in the 1890s.

Mohawk: a shaved head with a brush of hair one to six inches high running down the middle of the scalp. Originally worn by Mohawk Indians but revived by punk rockers in the 1980s.

pageboy: a style featuring bangs and hair falling straight to the sides with ends turned under.

pigtails: braids hanging on either side of the head.

pixie: a short cut characterized by points around the forehead and face.

pompadour: a style in which hair is swept up high from the forehead, popular in the early 1900s as the "Gibson Girl" look and revived in slightly different modes since.

poodle cut: a short, curly haircut, similar to a poodle's coat.

porcupine: a punk haircut characterized by long spikes or strands of hair standing on end down the middle of the head.

pulled back: a style in which the hair is pulled back and tied with a ribbon or held with a barrette.

punk: any Mohawk, porcupine, dyed, shaved, sculpted or spiked hair.

receding hairline: progressive balding, from front to back.

roach: hair brushed back to form a roll.

rooster mane: male cut characterized by hair gathered at the top from front to back, or a Mohawk style.

sculptured: hair styled with shaved-in designs, logos or initials. Also, moussed hair arranged in various fashions.

shag: a shaggy bob worn with bangs.

shock: bushy mass.

skinhead: a shaved head.

spikes: a punk style characterized by long spikes of moussed or gelled hair, sometimes dyed.

spit curl: a curl of hair kept together and attached to the face with saliva.

tail: style of the late 1980s and early 1990s in which a narrow sprig of hair is allowed to grow out from the back of the head and down the back.

tonsure: a fringed circle of hair surrounding a bald crown.

topknot: a knot tied at the crown of the head.

Veronica Lake: popular in the 1940s and again in the 1960s, a style characterized by the hair parted to one side to partially cover one eye; named after the actress who originated the look.

wedge: the wildly popular Dorothy Hamill look of the 1970s. The hair on the front and sides is the same length, with the back tapered close to the head.

widow's peak: hair tapering to a point on the forehead.

FACIAL HAIR

Beards

à la Souvaroff: a mustache/beard in which the mustache is joined to the sideburns and the chin is left clean-shaven.

anchor: a short, pointed beard worn at the edge of the chin with a fringe extending up to the center of the bottom lip.

Assyrian: a long beard with plaits or spiral curls.

barbiche: a small tuft of hair under the bottom lip. Also known as a barbula.

Belgrave: a neatly groomed, medium-length beard that may be cut round, square or with a point.

burnside: the mustache joined with the sideburns and the jaw left clean-shaven; named after General Ambrose Burnside in the nineteenth century.

cadiz: a pointed, medium-length beard, originating in Spain.

cathedral beard: a full, flowing beard that splits like a fish tail at the bottom, worn by the clergy in mid sixteenth to the seventeenth centuries.

ducktail: a long, slender, neatly-trimmed beard, reminiscent of the tail of a duck.

Dundreary whiskers: sideburns grown long and left to hang off the sides of the face while the chin is left clean-shaven.

fish-tail: See cathedral beard.

five o'clock shadow: subtle or light stubble growth found on most men's faces at the end of the day.

forked: a beard cut or combed into two branches or wisps. Also known as a swallowtail.

goatee: a small, pointed beard, resembling that of a goat.

grizzled, grizzly: gray or flecked with gray.

Imperial: a long tuft of hair extending down from beneath the lower lip; made famous by Napoleon III in 1839.

Jewish: a long, full, untrimmed beard, as that prescribed in the book of Leviticus. Also known as a Hebraic beard.

Lincolnesque: a medium-length beard worn with sideburns but no mustache; made famous by Abraham Lincoln.

Miami Vice: the unshaven look, more than five o'clock shadow but less than a beard, popularized by the 1980s cop show.

muttonchops: thick sideburns trimmed to resemble mutton chops.

Old Dutch: a short, square-cut beard with a clean-shaven upper and lower lip.

Olympian: a very long, thick beard.

paintbrush: a very small, pointed beard worn on the bottom of the chin, reminiscent of the tip of a paintbrush.

peach fuzz: light, pubescent whiskers.

pencil: a pencil-width of whiskers extending from the bottom lip to the chin.

Raleigh: a pointed beard with the facial portion closely cropped; named after Sir Walter Raleigh.

rat's nest: a descriptive term for an uncombed or ungroomed beard. Also described as a bird's nest.

Roman T: a small, rectangular chin tuft that, in conjunction with a rectangular mustache, forms the configuration of the letter *T*.

Satyric tuft: a chin tuft, named after Satyr, the half-goat, half-man from Greek mythology.

screw: a short, slender beard that is twisted or twined, popular in the seventeenth century. May be used to denote any twisted beard.

Shenandoah: a spade-shaped beard.

spade: a pointed or rounded beard, reminiscent of the shape of a spade.

square-cut: a medium or long beard cut square or flat on the bottom.

steel wool: a descriptive term for a tough, wiry beard.

stiletto: a long, slender, pointed beard.

swallowtail: a forked beard, reminiscent of the tail of a swallow.

tile: a long or short square-cut beard.

Trojan: a thick, curly beard of medium length.

Uncle Sam: the beard style worn by the U.S. cartoon figure.

Van Dyke: a short, pointed beard without sideburns.

Viking: any long, flowing beard reminiscent of the ancient Norsemen.

Mustaches

à la Souvaroff: a style characterized by a clean-shaven chin and a mustache joined to the sideburns.

boxcar: a rectangular style with square ends, like a railroad car.

chevron: an inverted *V*.

Clark Gable: a neat, thin line.

cookie duster: humorous descriptive term for a mustache.

Fu Manchu: long, thin drooping mustache worn with a narrow beard.

handlebar: a long, thick mustache with ends turned up to resemble the handlebars of a bicycle.

Hindenburg: a very long, thick mustache with turned-up ends.

horseshoe: an inverted *U* or horseshoe-like mustache that droops down over the chin.

Kaiser: a mustache with turned-up ends; popularized by Germany's Kaiser in 1914.

mistletoe: a narrow mustache in the configuration of two crescents, reminiscent of mistletoe leaves.

pencil line: a very narrow mustache, sometimes divided with a space at the center of the lip.

pyramid: a triangular mustache.

rat's nest: descriptive term for an unkempt mustache.

regent: a neat mustache resembling the letter *M* with rounded peaks.

Roman T: a style comprised of a rectangular mustache and a narrow chin tuft, forming the configuration of the letter *T*.

soupstrainer: See walrus.

square button: See toothbrush.

toothbrush: a short square or rectangle of bristles, as worn by Adolph Hitler and Charlie Chaplin.

walrus: a thick, huge mustache allowed to grow over the upper, and sometimes even the lower, lip. Humorously known as a soupstrainer.

waxed: any mustache with curled tips, twiddled and held together with wax.

wings: a neatly trimmed mustache resembling the wings of a bird.

wings of a B-52: a broad inverted *V*, like the wings of the classic bomber.

OTHER FACIAL FEATURES

Head Shapes

bullet-headed
egg-shaped
gibbous
high-domed
high forehead
hydrocephalic
inverted pear
low forehead
macrocephalic
microcephalic
moon
oval
pinhead
protruding brow ridges
round

Mouth

cruel
Cupid's bow
dour
dry line

firm
fishy
full ripe lips
humorous
misshapen
pallid
plum
protruding lips
puckered
rosebud
sensual
set in a permanent frown
set in permanent disapproval
veal-colored lips

Chin/Jaw

cleft chin
double chin
heavy jaw
lantern jaw
Neanderthal jaw
receding chin
round firm chin
slack-jawed
square jaw
wattled

Cheeks

apple
flabby
high cheekbones
high Slavic cheekbones

hollow
leathery
pendulous jowls
pouchy
rosy
ruddy

Teeth

buck teeth
Chiclet teeth
corn-kerneled
crooked
dentures
gap-toothed
horse-like
ill-fitting dentures
jagged
pearly
pitted with cavities
saw-toothed
small glistening white teeth
snaggle-toothed
tobacco-stained
yellow

FACIAL TYPES

Odd or Interesting Faces

aristocratic
baboon
beaver
bird-like

bloodhound
cadaverous
Cesar Romero
chinless
chipmunk
craggy
Cro-Magnon (primitive)
Cupid
deformed
disfigured
dour
droopy
ethereal
exotic
fierce
fish
ghoulish
gnome-like
gorilla
hag
harridan
hideous
homely
insect-like
Lincolnesque
misshapen
monkey
mousy
Neanderthal (protruding brow ridges and heavy jaw)
other-worldly
owlish
pig-nosed
plain

pop-eyed
prim
puckish
Quasimodo
rat-faced
regal
repulsive
slack-jawed
sleepy-eyed
ugly as a gourd
vole-faced

Big Faces

beefy
blowsy
bulldog
bullfrog
double-chinned
doughy
dumpling
Falstaffian
fleshy
fleshy wattle under the chin
heavy-jowled
horse
long-jawed

meaty

moon

plump

pouchy chipmunk cheeks

round

spherical

Attractive Faces

Adonis

angelic

Aphrodite

Apollo

baby-faced

bonny

boyish

cherubic

chiseled

comely

delicate

dimpled

distinguished

doll

elegant

ethereal (other-worldly)

feline

girlish

handsome (ruggedly, wolfishly, roguishly)

heart-shaped

high cheekbones

Nordic

nymph

pixie-faced

sculpted
square-jawed
sweetly expressive
symmetrical

Aged Faces

cadaverous
careworn
corn-kernel teeth
crow's feet
fleshy wattle
furrowed brow
gap-toothed
gaunt
haggard
hair sprouting from ears
hair sprouting from moles
hollowed cheekbones
hollows around the eyes
ill-fitting dentures
jaundiced
laugh lines
leathery complexion
lined like old shoe leather
liver-spotted
mirthful crinkles about the eyes
mottled complexion
parchment skin
pendulous skin folds
prune-faced
rawboned
rheumy eyes

sagging jowls
scalded-milk skin
skullish grin
squint lines
sunken eye sockets
timeworn
toothless pucker
tremulous jaw
weathered complexion
withered
wizened
yellowed scleras

BODY TYPES

Attractive Bodies

athletic
buxom
compact
curvaceous
delicate
diminutive
fit
full-figured
hourglass
iron-muscled
lean
leggy
lissome
lithe
petite
rippling

rock-hard
rugged
sinewy
sleek
slim
slinky
split high (long-legged)
stacked
statuesque
strapping
svelte
tall
thin
toned
waspish (wasp-waisted)
willowy
wiry

Big Bodies

Amazonian
barrel-chested
barrel-shaped
beefy
big as a bull
big as a draft horse
big as an ox
big as a refrigerator
big-boned
blubbery
bovine
brawny
broad in the beam

Brobdingnagian (gigantic, as in the fabled inhabitants of Brob-
  dingnag in Swift's *Gulliver's Travels*)

burly

chubby

colossal

corpulent

deplorably fat

disgracefully fat

doughy

dumpling

elephantine

fleshy

full-figured

Humpty Dumpty

lavishly endowed

lumpy

obese

paunchy

pear-shaped

plump

portly

pot-bellied

pudgy

roly-poly

spherical

squat

stocky

stout

sumo wrestler

thickset

unequivocably fat

wrestler

Aged Bodies

asthenic

bow-spined

dowager's hump

edema (swelling in lower legs and feet)

gaunt

gnarled fingers (rheumatoid arthritis)

haggard

hunched

malnourished

osteoporotic (osteoporosis is characterized by brittle bones,
  often resulting in broken hips in older women)

palsied

reedy

rickety

shriveled

spindly

stooped

withered

Miscellaneous Body Types

anorexic

bullnecked

deformed

dwarf

fire-plug

gangling

hunchbacked

lanky

midget

muscular and compact as a pit bull

muscular as linguine

oafish

runty

scrawny

slight (could slip through a flute and not sound a note)

spare

stubby

thin as a broomstick

towering

whippet thin

BODY PARTS

Necks

bobbing Adam's apple

bullnecked

corded

delicate

flabby

leathery

slender

swan-like

tough as beef jerky

wattled

Shoulders

bony

delicate shoulders

drooping (head sunk into drooping shoulders)

massive oarsman's shoulders

round shoulders

square shoulders

stoop-shouldered

Hands and Arms

arms like a gibbon
arthritic, gnarled fingers
ballooning biceps
bony, stick-like arms
callused fingers
chapped hands
clammy hands
claw-like fingers
corded arm muscles
flabby arms
greasy, oily hands
hairy hands
hands like hams
long, delicate hands
manicured hands
polydactyl (having more than the normal number of fingers
    and toes)
pudgy hands
red and scoured hands
stringy muscles
stubby fingers
work-swollen, banged-up hands
wrestler's arms

Chest

barrel-chested
caved-in chest
chiseled pecs
defined pecs
hairless
hairy

Breasts

bosomy
buoyant
busty
buxom
flat-chested (proverbial bee stings)
globular
jutting cones
lavishly endowed
melon-breasted
overdeveloped
sag-chested
top-heavy
underdeveloped
withered
wizened

Belly

beer-bellied
beer keg
blubbery
chiseled abdomen
flabby
flat
fleshy
iron stomach muscles
love handles
middle-aged spread
muttonous
overflowing beltline
paunchy
pendulous

plump
pot-bellied
rippling
spare tire
spherical
swinging belly
toned
V-cut abdomen
washboard stomach

Legs and Hips

bandy-legged
bowlegged
bulging quadriceps
hourglass curves
knock-kneed
leggy (split high)
pearlike bulge at the hips
slab-thighed
spindly
wasp-waisted
wide-hipped

Feet

club-footed
flat-footed
pigeon-toed
polydactyl (having more than the normal number of toes)
swollen with edema

Voices

bass
bellowing

booming
breathy
cackling
childlike
cracking (adolescent/pubescent)
croaking
cultured
deep
drawling
droning
falsetto
faltering
feeble
flat
fluting
gravel
guttural
harsh
hoarse
hoarse flute
hollow
husky
inflectionless
lilting
lisping
megaphonic
monotone
nasal twang
piercing
ponderous
ponticello (boy's change of voice at puberty)
powerful
purring

quavering

rasping

reedy

resonant

robust

scabrous

sensuous

Shakespearean actor's

sharp

shrill

sing-song

soothing

spluttering

squawking

squeaky

stentorian (from Stentor, a Greek herald celebrated for his
    powerful voice)

subterranean

sultry

thick

thin

throaty

thunderous

tobacco-roughened

tremulous

velvety

warbling

well-bred

wheezing

whining

whiskey-voiced

2

Personality/ Identity

PERSONALITY TRAITS INVENTORY

Introvert

prefers one's own company to others

would rather read a book than attend party

holds back when placed in new situations and proceeds
 cautiously

quiet

enjoys and seeks out solitude

introspective

doesn't like being in spotlight

withdrawn

wary

reserved

aloof

unexpressive

independent

autonomous
discreet
unassuming
inhibited
isolated
monastic
private
nonverbal
shy
soft-spoken
self-effacing
self-conscious
analytical
has and wants only one or two close friends
needs time to think
philosophical
deep-thinking

Extrovert

friendly
gregarious
outgoing
party-goer
warm
confident
loquacious
verbal
expressive
animated
assertive
show-offy
exhibitionistic

immodest
uninhibited
has and needs many friends
loud
vocal
doesn't like being alone
seeks out social events
spontaneous
conversational

Cold

undemonstrative
stiffens when touched
shrinks from one's touch
aloof
distant
remote
detached
emotionless
humorless
speaks in monotone
unsmiling
dour
thick-skinned
rude
forbidding
hard, pinched facial expression
grim
misanthropic
stony-faced
needs extra body space
unforgiving

uncompassionate
heartless
brutal
indifferent
hands bunched into fists
no eye contact
piercing, impolite eye contact

Domineering/Overbearing

finishes sentences for others
interrupts frequently
stands intimidatingly close to others when speaking (no re-
    spect for body space of others)
glaring
withering stare
swaggers
macho posturing
imperious body language
peers down nose imperiously
loud
barks orders
take-over, officious manner
verbally or physically abusive
disrespects underlings
scathing insults at underlings
bossy
dogmatic
willful
pigheaded
stubborn
rules with an iron fist
high-handed
lordly

messianic

suffers from "expertitis," will not listen to advice of others and eventually suffers consequences

enjoys making people feel uncomfortable and seeing them in timidated

Nervous/Shy/Submissive

coughs, clears throat a lot

fidgets

runs hands through hair a lot

clenches jaw a lot

darts eyes back and forth

saucer-eyed

voice strained

trembling

facial tics

jangles change in pocket

deferential

smiling

overly polite

blushes easily

stutters

stammers

voice croaks

palms and underarms sweaty

averts eyes, avoids eye contact

blinks a lot

affects an elaborately casual manner

affects an elaborately nonchalant manner

apologetic

equivocal

fawning

mealy-mouthed

wishy-washy
solicitous
insecure
sensitive
over-sensitive
self-conscious

Sad Sack/Gloomy Gus

mopes
hang-dog expression
sighs a lot
slouches
slumps in chair
"poor-me" martyr attitude
"life stinks" attitude
low self-esteem
pessimistic
never happy unless miserable
dissatisfied
cheerless
pained expression
pensive look
somber
cynical
unsmiling
wistful
stick-in-the-mud
sullen
maudlin
morbid
thinks too much about death
humorless

glum
sees the bad in everything

Intelligent

skeptical
discerning
analytical
logical
thoughtful
insightful
creative
suspicious
well-read
rational
perceptive
shrewd
inquisitive
accomplished
artful
cerebral
bookish
cautious
clever
prepared
versatile
savvy
not easily fooled
cynical
worldly
great insight into one's own and others' behavior
experienced
well-schooled

inventive

wise

discriminating

open-minded

far-sighted

deep

complex

questions authority

unaffected by peer pressure

Ignorant

bovine

bumbling

gullible

naive

does not question authority

affected by peer pressure

easily fooled

illiterate

thinks reading is for nerds

dropped out of school

believes wholeheartedly in astrology, psychics, UFOs, etc.

little insight into one's own or others' behavior

easily taken in by cons or sales gimmicks

taken advantage of by others

sophomoric sense of humor

oblivious

inarticulate

uses street language, unpolished speech

doesn't think things through

doesn't always think of consequences for actions

opinions of politics and current events based on faulty or deficient information

unthinkingly prejudiced
unthinkingly racist
unthinkingly sexist/chauvinistic
stereotypes everyone
impulsive
reckless
incautious, unaware of natural hazards of everyday life
artless
doesn't think before speaking
gives glib, facile advice

Boring

talks endlessly about oneself
hogs conversation
talks about things others cannot relate to
babbles
doesn't listen
is oblivious to the social cues of others
taciturn
doesn't talk at all
brags about accomplishments of self and family members
uninformed about current events
has no opinions
wishy-washy
mealy-mouthed
speaks in monotone
no sense of humor
one-dimensional
tiresome
dresses in one-color, conservative clothing day after day
never changes routine
eats at the same restaurants, orders the same dish every time

afraid of change
afraid to take risks
maintains the same routine for a lifetime
overly agreeable
avoids conflict
never raises voice
never gets angry or passionate about anything

Eccentric

nonconforming
weird
original
individualistic
doesn't care what others think
wears wild or unconventional clothing
walks or rides bicycle everywhere
odd beliefs
does what others are afraid to do
radical
fanatical
mad
insane
crazed
deranged
psychotic
neurotic
obsessed
manic
excessive
extravagant
quirky
wild-eyed

scatterbrained

enjoys shocking people with unconventional behavior

attention-seeking behavior

believes his is sane behavior in an insane world

hermit-like

Charming/Well-Bred

suave

debonair

gracious

knows what to do in every social situation (savoir faire)

makes people feel at ease

makes people feel good about themselves

polite

smooth

poise of worldly experience

gentlemanly

ladylike

tactful

confident

warm

friendly

unobjectionably flirtatious

complimentary

flattering

congenial

convivial

personable

romantic

likes to touch

disarming

captivating

good-humored
diplomatic
charismatic
well-groomed
clean and neat
fashionable
sexually attractive
winning smile
steady but warm eye contact
thoughtful
considerate

Devious/Conniving/Evil

plotting
wily
pulling strings
venomous
unprincipled
false
fraudulent
artful
underhanded
manipulative
lying
backstabbing
acts angelic/saintly/innocent
wide-eyed innocence
two-faced
sneaky
self-serving
evasive
power-hungry

avaricious

gold-digging

disarming charm

charismatic

Svengali-like charisma

smoldering sexuality

opposite sex finds despicable—but is inexplicably attracted to sexually

womanizing

cheats on spouse

suspicious of the actions of others

traitorous

uses people

paranoid

shameless

corrupt

deceitful

unsympathetic to others

lacking conscience

sociopathic

ruthless

can locate the chink in the strongest person's armor

predatory expression

hungry look

stalking look

confident

bold

controlling

dominant

Annoying

know-it-all

sarcastic

sardonic

stick-in-the-mud

gloomy Gus

wet blanket

cracks jokes at expense of other people

tells offensive jokes in mixed company

vulgar

flirtatious in offensive manner

harasses others sexually

tattletale

whining

whining nasal voice

shallow

insensitive to the feelings of others

inconsiderate

sophomoric behavior

loud

macho posturing

catty

gossipy

smug

self-righteous

holier-than-thou

judgmental

glib

rude

discourteous

inappropriate

wise-assed

insincere

pretentious

phony

affected
talks about oneself constantly
hogs conversation
doesn't listen
interrupts
outshines everyone in room
hogs the spotlight
corrects others constantly
overly proper
anal retentive
does everything by the book
prudish
Victorian
puritanical
officious
nosy
offers advice when none wanted or called for
critical
nagging
needling
badgering
second-guessing
Monday-morning quarterbacking
blaming everyone but oneself for troubles
unjust sense of entitlement because society has hurt one in
some way

Puritanical/Proper

goody-goody
politically correct
feels superior to others
sees others as immoral heathens
scrupulously moral

well-mannered

upright

chaste

squeaky clean

stiff

rigid

religious

overly religious

overly guided by Bible

blinded by the authority of the church

holier-than-thou

self-righteous

sanctimonious

quotes Bible or etiquette book chapter and verse

starchy

conservative

wears drab, conservative, unsexy clothes

prim

refuses to laugh at risqué humor

strict

stern

judgmental

prissy

modest

law-abiding

hard-working

ethical

honest

goes to church every Sunday

doesn't drink alcohol, smoke cigarettes, or have sex in broad
  daylight

knows what's best for others

easily offended or shocked

believes in censorship

thinks people who smoke or drink are bad

Happy/Jovial

good-humored

easygoing

joking

eyes are mirthful crescents

laughs easily

funny

face aglow with good cheer

lighthearted

relaxed

smiling, grinning

friendly

warm

cheerful

optimistic

buoyant

jaunty

devil-may-care

happy-go-lucky

childlike

silly

fun-loving

contented

doesn't let bad news get him down

philosophical about let-downs

doesn't dwell on negative

"live and let live" attitude

playful

blithe

carefree

live-for-today
animated
effervescent
bubbly
vivacious
energetic
bright-eyed
robust health
sings
whistles
hums

Type A

hostile
hard-driving
impatient
cynical
thinks everyone else is stupid
hates being late, shows up early
can't tolerate when others are late
hot reacting
fast driving
angry, frustrated driver
easily stressed
irritable
fidgety
unable to relax
drums fingers impatiently
aggressive
easily aggravated
belligerent
pugnacious

fuming
hot-blooded
short-fused
volcanic temper
temperamental
restless
hyper

Type B

relaxed
laid-back
easygoing
long-fused
patient
cool-headed
mild
even-tempered
unaggressive
noncombative
passive
pacifistic
sedate
devil-may-care
carefree
calm

Mentally Ill

delusional
suffers from hallucinations
irrational behavior
glassy-eyed from psychotropic drugs
manic-depressive

hyper
depressed
neurotic
obsessive
compulsive
insanely jealous
phobic
unstable
homicidal
sociopathic
delusions of grandeur
thinks he is Christ
thinks he is endowed with superhuman powers
paranoid
believes he is being persecuted
believes he is being followed
believes CIA is bugging telephone
believes he is receiving messages over television
believes he is an alien
panic attacks
anorexic
bulimic
suicidal

Alcoholic/Substance Abuser

in denial about substance abuse
denies being addicted
thoughts center around booze or drugs
hiding booze or drugs in several locations to ensure never to
  be without
sickly
fights with spouse about addiction
dysfunctional

irresponsible
steals in order to buy drugs
secretive
hangs out at bars
drinks alone
eyes often red and bloodshot
slurred speech
dull expression

Sexual/Flirtatious

slinky body language
scorching eye contact
cow eyes
demure
coy
suggestive talk or behavior
uses double entendres
touches a lot
dresses provocatively
teasing behavior
promiscuous

Childish/Adolescent

sophomoric sense of humor
bathroom humor
silly
giggling
immature
irresponsible
fun-loving
impulsive
poor judgment

fickle
callow
naive
innocent
wide-eyed
unrealistic
shortsighted
melodramatic
ruled by peer pressure
know-it-all
kooky
infantile
practical jokes
clowning
reckless
risk-taking
false bravado
awkward

Strong/Brave

risk-taking
adventurous
stoic
won't admit pain
unblinking
unflinching
thick-skinned
virile
manly
macho
courageous
gritty

daring
brash
powerful
doesn't quit in the face of adversity
heroic
self-esteem depends on outward show of strength
disgusted by weakness
leadership skills
won't admit softer feelings
not in touch with softer feelings
won't admit fear

BAD HABITS/VICES

oversleeps
overworks
drinks too much
smokes
bites fingernails
picks nose in public
eats with mouth open
leaves toenail clippings all over floor
shaves and leaves whiskers in sink
doesn't put the toilet seat down
doesn't flush the toilet
farts in public
interrupts people talking
grinds teeth
cracks knuckles
smokes pot
sniffs cocaine
smokes crack
does heroin

obsessed with sex

drools

laughs too loud when nervous

laughs too much when nervous

whistles when nervous

hums when nervous

leaves dirty clothes all over floor

falls asleep in clothes

gambles

drums fingers when impatient

speeds in car

ignores yield signs

tailgates

clears throat too much when nervous

leaves lights and TV on when leaving house

has to check stove or iron five times to make sure they're turned off

takes nap in middle of work day

cracks jokes at expense of other people

forgets a lot

loses keys often

eats too often at fast-food restaurants

eats soups and other foods straight out of the can without heating

neglects pets

forgets to comb hair before going out

doesn't always brush teeth

picks fights

wears too much perfume or cologne

checks self in mirror too much

shouts at and debates with the TV

watches too much TV

watches too much sports

talks on the phone too much
kicks the cat when angry
swears too much
drinks milk out of container
stands people up
fishes for compliments
fishes for sympathy for numerous physical ailments
tips too much
doesn't tip at all
eats greasy foods with fingers
wolfs down food
burps loudly in public
coughs without covering mouth
finishes people's sentences for them
offers advice when it's not wanted
finishes everyone else's meal for them
snacks too much
chews gum too much
rolls over and goes to sleep after sex
litters
shoplifts small items
parks in handicapped space
nags people
plays "one-upsmanship" with others
hogs conversation
apologizes for everything
thanks people too much

PSYCHOLOGICAL/PSYCHIATRIC PROBLEMS

Bella
Swan,
anyone?
Agreed!
stupid

accident-prone: an unconscious need for attention manifesting itself through an unusual number of accidents or mishaps.

achiria: a fit of hysteria in which the victim falsely believes he has lost one or both of his hands.

aeroneurosis: a restless anxiety experienced by airplane pilots.

alethia: dwelling, to a neurotic degree, on the past.

amnesia: loss of memory, brought on by physical or mental trauma.

anaclisis: a neurotic attachment to one who is reminiscent of one's mother or father during childhood.

anal retentive: picky-neat or overly ordered, meticulous and obstinate.

animality: the expression of innate animal behaviors; vestigial primitive behavior.

anomie: feelings of alienation and not belonging to society.

anorexia nervosa: an eating disorder born out of a fear of growing fat, characterized by extreme dieting to the point of emaciation, most frequently seen in teenaged girls and young women.

antisocial personality: a disordered personality characterized by impulsiveness, lack of conscience or guilt feelings, and a complete disregard for others. Formerly known as a sociopath or psychopath.

anxiety: fear, nervousness or apprehension caused by a real or imagined source.

aphagia: inability to eat.

aphasia: loss of speech or the facility for understanding speech as a result of brain damage or disease, or mental trauma.

asocial: unsociable, disinterested in others.

astasia-abasia: a fit of hysteria in which the victim falsely believes he can no longer stand up or walk.

atavism: regressing to a primitive state of mind or behavior.

attention deficit disorder: a disorder, often identified in school-aged children, characterized by impulsiveness and the inability to pay attention.

bestiality: the act or fantasy of having sex with animals.

borderline personality disorder: an unstable personality characterized by impulsiveness, unpredictability and suicidal tendencies.

bulimia: an eating disorder characterized by alternating binging and forced vomiting, most frequently seen in teenaged girls and young women.

cardioneurosis: a neurotic fear of having a heart attack. Symptoms include perceived chest pains, palpitations and shortness of breath.

cataphasia: repetition of the same word or phrase over and over.

catatonia: a motionless or mute stupor, a syndrome of schizophrenia.

compensation: an ego-protection mechanism through which a person who is inferior or deficient in one area tries to become superior in another to make up for it.

compulsion: any irrational or ritualistic behavior carried out repetitively, such as compulsive hand-washing.

compulsive personality: a personality characterized by extreme conscientiousness, rigidity, anxiety and an obsession for trivial details.

conversion: the unconscious process through which mental stress is manifested through a physical, physiologic or psychological symptom.

coprophilia: an abnormal fascination with feces.

decompensation: psychological deterioration due to long-term or severe stress.

delirium tremens: hallucinations, tremors and paranoia caused by alcohol poisoning.

delusion: a false belief about oneself or the world. Believing oneself to be Jesus Christ or Superman is a delusion.

delusions of grandeur: falsely believing one is greater, more powerful or more important than one is in reality.

dementia: behavior disturbances and loss of intellectual sharpness due to a brain disorder, often associated with aging.

dependent personality disorder: a personality characterized by passivity, helplessness, and dependence on other people.

depression: feelings of sadness that may be severe, chronic and debilitating.

echolalia: a brain disorder in which the victim repeats the words of others.

exhibitionism: exposing oneself in public for sexual gratification. Also, a tendency to show off or call attention to oneself through various means.

explosive disorder: a disorder characterized by violent outbursts.

explosive personality: personality characterized by explosive outbursts followed by periods of remorse.

fetishism: a sexual attraction to inanimate objects, such as shoes or jewelry.

free-floating anxiety: vague feelings of anxiety without an apparent cause or stimulus.

fugue state: a temporary flight from reality; amnesia.

hallucination: a phantom or false perception; perceiving something or someone, such as a ghost, that isn't there.

hallucinosis: auditory, visual and tactile hallucinations brought on by withdrawal from severe alcohol abuse.

hebephrenia: a form of schizophrenia characterized by regressive behavior and a perpetual silly grin.

histrionic personality: a personality characterized by attention-seeking behaviors, overdependency, egocentricity and excitability.

hyperactivity: a disorder of childhood characterized by fidgety or excessive activity and a failure to complete tasks.

hyperphagia: pathological overeating.

hyperventilation: a symptom of anxiety characterized by rapid breathing accompanied by the feeling of shortness of breath, light-headedness and palpitations, usually cured quickly by breathing into a paper bag.

hypochondriasis: excessive worry or dread over being sick; dwelling on one's aches and pains and overall health. Sufferers often report a variety of symptoms, most frequently difficulty in swallowing, shortness of breath, chest pains, bloating, cramps and insomnia. The disorder is almost always associated with depression.

hysteria: a neurotic state characterized by excessive anxiety and excitability, and sometimes amnesia, hallucinations or other mental symptoms.

inadequate personality: one who is socially and emotionally inept.

inferiority complex: low self-esteem and feeling that one is inferior to others.

Korsakoff's psychosis: distorted thinking and memory loss caused by alcohol.

logomania: excessive or ceaseless talk.

logorrhea: excessive and irrational talk.

malingerer: one who feigns illness in order to get out of responsibility or work.

mania: irrational excitement, euphoria or elation accompanied by flighty or grandiose ideas, hyperactivity; the manic phase of manic-depressive illness.

mania: an excessive enthusiasm or obsession for something or someone; craze.

Mania Types

alcohol	dipsomania
animals	zoomania
bathing, washing	ablutomania
books	bibliomania
cats	ailuromania
children	pedomania
Christ, believing one is	theomania
dancing	choreomania

```
death ..................................... necromania
demon possession .................. demonomania
dogs ...................................... cynomania
eating .................................... sitomania
fire ....................................... pyromania
flowers .................................. anthomania
food ...................................... phagomania
genius, believing one is .......... sophomania
horses ................................... hippomania
kill, urge to ........................... dacnomania
money .................................... chrematomania
nakedness .............................. gymnomania
night ..................................... noctimania
pleasure ................................. hedonomania
religion .................................. entheomania
sex ........................................ aphrodisiomania, nympho-
                                           mania, erotomania
sleep ..................................... hypnomania
solitude ................................. automania
stealing ................................. kleptomania
sun ....................................... heliomania
talking .................................. logomania
wealth ................................... plutomania
wine ...................................... oinomania
women ................................... gynemania
woods .................................... hylomania
work ..................................... ergomania
```

manic: excited; suffering from mania.

manic-depressive psychosis: a disease characterized by mood swings, from normal to depressed or from normal to euphoric, or a combination of both.

martyrdom: "poor me syndrome," a neurotic behavior in which one takes on too much responsibility, or blames oneself for everything negative that happens, in order to elicit sympathy from others.

masochism: deriving sexual stimulation from being hit, dominated or mistreated by another.

megalomania: delusions of grandeur; false belief that one is greater, wealthier or more powerful than one really is.

misanthropy: a hatred for people.

misogyny: hatred of women.

multiple personality: the manifestation of more than one personality by an individual as a dissociative reaction to extreme trauma, abuse, etc.

Munchausen's Syndrome: a rare disorder in which people inflict injury or illness (sometimes by taking drugs or too many laxatives) onto themselves in order to get attention at a medical facility, named after Baron Karl von Munchausen, an eighteenth-century German soldier known for his tall tales. A related disorder is Munchausen's Syndrome by Proxy, in which mothers fake illnesses or injuries in their children, sometimes by forcing them to take drugs or laxatives or by smothering or some other means, and then try to convince the medical community that the illnesses are real.

narcissism: excessive self-interest or self-love; self-centeredness.

necrophilism: sexual intercourse with a corpse; deriving sexual pleasure from a corpse.

obsessive-compulsive disorder: a neurotic disorder characterized by irresistible urges, thoughts and rituals repeated again and again, such as checking ten times to make sure the front door is locked before leaving for work.

Oedipus Complex: sexual attraction of a boy to his mother with accompanying feelings of hostility toward his father. The female version is known as the *Electra Complex*.

panic disorder: a thought disorder, sometimes aggravated by a heart rhythm defect or other physical problem, in which anxiety spirals out of control. Signs of a panic attack include hyperventilation, racing heart, oxygen hunger and a feeling of impending doom. Such attacks can often be subdued by breathing into a paper bag.

paranoia: a delusional state in which one believes he is being persecuted by others. Also known as a persecution complex.

paranoid schizophrenia: schizophrenia with marked delusions of persecution.

passive-aggressive personality: a manipulative, immature personality characterized by hostility, petulance and fault-finding. One suffering from the disorder may express power through passive means, such as by being chronically late or forgetting. They may also alternate between being overly dependent and overly independent. A passive-aggressive person placed in a work setting frequently destroys morale through childish or antagonistic behavior.

pedophilia: sexual relations between an adult and a child; deriving sexual pleasure from a child.

phantosmia: odor hallucinations.

phobia: an irrational fear of a particular person, place or thing.

Phobia Types

animals	zoophobia
blood	hemophobia
blushing	erythrophobia
bridges	gephyrophobia
burial alive	taphephobia
cancer	cancer phobia
cats	ailurophobia
children	pedophobia
confinement in small places	claustrophobia
crowds	demophobia
dark	nyctophobia
dead bodies/death	necrophobia, thanatophobia
depths	bathophobia
dogs	cynophobia
eating	phagophobia
everything	panphobia

failure	kakorrhaphiophobia
fire	pyrophobia
flood	antlophobia
foreigners	xenophobia
ghosts	phasmophobia
heights	acrophobia
insects	acaraphobia, entomophobia
knives	aichmophobia
marriage	gamophobia
medicine	pharmacophobia
men	androphobia
mice	musophobia
night	nyctophobia
number 13	triskaidekaphobia
ocean	thalassophobia
old age	gerontophobia
open spaces	agoraphobia
poison	toxicophobia
responsibility	hypengyophobia
ridicule	catagelophobia
sex	coitophobia, genophobia
sin, committing a	peccatiphobia
sleep	hypnophobia
snakes	ophidiophobia
solitude	autophobia
speaking	lalophobia
spiders	arachneophobia
strangers	xenophobia
sunlight	heliophobia
thunderstorms	astraphobia, brontophobia
touched, being	haptephobia
women	gynephobia
work	ergophobia

pica: abnormal craving for or eating of unusual foods, such as dirt or laundry detergent, seen in the emotionally disturbed and sometimes in pregnant women.

post-traumatic stress disorder: anxiety, depression and other stress symptoms that manifest themselves weeks, months or even years after living through a traumatic event.

pressured speech: rapid speech accelerating out of control, so that words are sometimes jumbled or unintelligible.

pseudocyesis: a delusion that one is pregnant when one is not.

psychogenic pain disorder: the manifestation of mental stress through physical aches and pains, which may be chronic or severe.

psychophysiological disorder: any physical illness that can be traced to a psychological cause. Also known as psychosomatic disorder.

psychosis: severe mental illness characterized by one or more mental disturbances, such as delusions or hallucinations.

regression: behaving or thinking primitively or childishly.

repression: blocking out unpleasant thoughts or traumatic memories.

retrograde amnesia: forgetting all the details of events that took place immediately before a traumatic episode.

SAD (Seasonal Affective Disorder): a form of depression thought to be brought on by diminishing sunlight in the autumn or early winter, with an improvement in mood in spring. Sometimes treated with artificial lighting.

sadism: deriving sexual pleasure from hurting or dominating someone.

satyriasis: an insatiable and abnormal desire for sex in men.

schizoid personality: a personality characterized by extreme shyness or aloofness; extreme introversion born out of the fear of being hurt by others.

schizophrenia: a psychosis characterized by distorted thinking, delusions, hallucinations and a range of bizarre behaviors.

shell shock: combat neurosis, characterized by jumpiness, insomnia and an inability to relax. Also known as battle fatigue.

split personality: See multiple personality.

superiority complex: a disorder in which one acts superior but actually feels inferior.

tachylogia: rapid and excessive speech.

transsexualism: feeling like a female in a male's body or vice versa. Sufferers feel they were destined to be of the gender other than the one they are. They report feeling "trapped" in the wrong body and often seek surgical correction. Transsexuals may wear the clothing of the opposite sex but, unlike transvestites, they do not derive sexual gratification from it. They usually suffer from a number of psychological problems, often due to a lack of acceptance by others.

transvestism: emotional or sexual gratification derived through wearing clothes of the opposite sex. The gratification is usually increased if the clothes are worn in public. Some transvestites are homosexual, but many are heterosexual married men with otherwise normal sex lives.

trichotillomania: compulsive hair pulling. Sufferers pull out hair from the scalp, eyebrows, eyelashes or elsewhere, often leaving glaring bald spots. Most sufferers are women.

voyeurism: deriving sexual pleasure from watching the sex acts of others.

zoosadism: deriving sexual pleasure from hurting animals.

SELECTED DISEASES, DISORDERS AND AFFLICTIONS

AIDS: Acquired Immune Deficiency Syndrome, caused by HIV (human immunodeficiency virus) that produces a breakdown in the body's natural immune system. The disease leaves the patient vulnerable to a host of infections and some forms of cancer, and it usually ends in death within ten years. The virus is most often spread by sexual contact or through IV drug use.

albinism: a genetic defect affecting melanin metabolism in the skin and eyes, or in the eyes alone. Victims typically have very pale skin (turning pinkish with age) that is highly susceptible to skin cancer and other forms of sun damage. Pupils are equally sensitive to sunlight and are frequently reddish in color. Hair may be white or yellowish, sometimes turning straw-colored with age. A person with albinism is strongly advised not to venture into the outdoors without sunscreen, protective clothing and dark glasses. The disorder is nearly three times more prevalent among African Americans than whites.

allergic rhinitis: allergy, sometimes called hay fever, suffered by more than 20 million Americans. It is commonly induced by such airborne allergens as tree pollens (in spring), grass pollens (in summer) and ragweed pollens (in the fall). Some suffer the allergy year-round, reacting not only to pollens but to house dust, animal dander and mold as well. Predominant symptoms include sneezing, runny nose or nasal congestion, sinus pain, and itchy, watery eyes. Some symptoms can be treated with antihistamines.

anaphylaxis: a severe reaction to an allergen or antigen, causing massive release of histamine. If not treated immediately with an injection of epinephrine, the reaction can swell the upper respiratory tract, cutting off breathing and causing death. Symptoms include a feeling of impending doom, sweating, sneezing, hives, shortness of breath or wheezing, severe stomach cramps and nausea. Substances most often triggering the reaction in allergic individuals include penicillin, bee venom, nuts, eggs and some seafoods. Those diagnosed with such acute sensitivity usually carry their own epinephrine injection kit.

angina pectoris: chest pain caused by a deficiency of blood flow to the heart, a symptom of heart or coronary artery disease.

appendicitis: inflammation of the appendix caused by obstruction and infection. Symptoms include pain in the upper right abdomen, eventually moving to the lower right abdomen, accompanied by anorexia and some vomiting, and a temperature of 99 to 102° F. Notably, the stomach becomes rigid, much like a board. The disease is always fatal unless treated.

asthma: a chronic condition marked by episodic breathing distress triggered by allergens such as pollen, animal dander and house dust, by infection or by emotional stress. Most-pronounced symptoms include shortness of breath, chest tightness with a feeling of suffocation, and wheezing. Half of all asthma cases begin under the age of ten. About 5,000 people die of severe asthma attacks each year.

astrocytoma: common brain tumor. Symptoms include headaches, seizures, nausea and behavior changes, with a survival rate of 6 to 7½ years.

basal cell epithelioma: a common, slow-growing, malignant skin tumor usually found in light-skinned people over the age of 40. Because the tumor is most often associated with long-term sun exposure, the most typical site is the face. Treatments include surgical removal, irradiation, curettage or drug therapy.

borborygmus: loud stomach rumblings.

breast cancer: the most common form of potentially fatal cancer among women. Usually found after age 35, breast cancer is most prevalent among women with a family history of the disease, women who have had long menstrual cycles, and women who first became pregnant after age 35. Signs of the cancer include a lump or mass in the breast, change in breast size, thickening or ulceration of breast skin, itching or burning in breast, and breast discharge when not lactating. Treatment includes lumpectomy, mastectomy, chemotherapy and radiation therapy.

cervical cancer: a common form of cancer in women between the ages of 30 and 50. Early stages, when the disease is most treatable, are without symptoms. Later stages are marked by abnormal vaginal bleeding, discharge and pain, accompanied by weight loss and anemia.

colorectal cancer: a common, slow-growing cancer, curable in most cases if caught early. Symptoms include abdominal pain, pressure and cramps, black, tarry stools, diarrhea, pallor, weakness and weight loss.

concussion: a variety of symptoms, such as amnesia, vomiting, headache, dizziness and irritability, caused by a strong blow to the head. Victims typically recover in 24 to 48 hours.

constipation: from poor or low fiber diet.

corns: hard, painful growths, usually appearing on the toes, caused by friction.

cystic fibrosis: the most common fatal congenital disease among white children. Half the children with the disease die by age 16; few survive beyond 30. The disease is characterized by pancreatic malfunction, frequent respiratory infections and sweat gland disfunction. Sufferers may wheeze, have a dry (nonproductive) cough and shortness of breath. They often have a barrel chest, cyanosis and clubbing of the fingers and toes. Death is usually brought on by pneumonia or emphysema.

deviated septum: a condition in which the thin wall of cartilage separating the two nasal passages grows abnormally or is misshapen through trauma and blocks or partially blocks one passage. People with deviated septums suffer from more headaches and sinusitis and may have a nasal voice.

Down's Syndrome: a chromosome aberration causing mental retardation, heart defects and Mongoloid facial features.

elephant man's disease: formally known as neurofibromatosis or Von Recklinghausen's disease, a genetic, developmental disorder of the muscles, bones, skin and nervous system affecting approximately 100,000 Americans. Its most obvious symptoms are external tumor or nodule growth (neurofibromas), café-au-lait-colored cutaneous lesions, scoliosis, spina bifida, neurologic damage and hypertension. Treatment includes corrective and cosmetic surgery.

epilepsy: a seizure disorder caused by electrical disturbances in the brain, affecting 1 to 2 percent of the population. The disorder produces two types of seizures: grand mal seizures, which begin with an "aura" or premonition of something about to happen, with the patient first crying out and then collapsing into unconsciousness, followed by stiffening of the body, spasms, tongue-biting and labored breathing that may last as long as five minutes; and petite mal seizures (usually occurring in children), which cause a change in the level of consciousness, blinking or rolling of the eyes, a blank stare and mouth movements. Petite mal seizures last only one to ten seconds but without treatment can occur up to 100 times per day. Drug therapy and sometimes surgery are employed to treat the disorder.

flatulence: intestinal gas from a diet high in beans and vegetables, or from swallowed air from chewing gum.

gallstones: formally known as cholelithiasis, gallstones are calculi (concretions of mineral salts around organic matter) that form in the gallbladder and are responsible for a large number of hospitalizations each year. The hallmark symptom is a gallbladder attack, usually occurring after a rich, fatty meal, causing severe pain in the upper right abdomen that sometimes spreads to the back and chest. Other signs are sour belches, indigestion, nausea, vomiting and flatulence. Cure rate is high with various treatments, including surgery.

glioblastoma multiforme: highly malignant, fast-growing brain tumor that frequently reaches massive proportions before detection, appearing most often in men between 50 and 60 years of age. Typical survival time is six months to two years. Symptoms include nausea, vomiting, headaches, seizures, visual defects and abnormal reflexes.

halitosis: bad breath.

heart attack: a deficiency or blockage of blood flow to the heart, causing crushing chest pains or pain in the left arm, shortness of breath, and a feeling of impending doom. About half of all heart attacks are fatal.

heartburn: reflux of stomach acid or stomach contents up into the esophagus after a meal, causing diffuse, burning chest pain that can be relieved by antacids.

hemophilia: a potentially fatal, genetic bleeding disorder caused by a deficiency of clotting agents. The hallmark of the disorder is abnormal or excessive bleeding with trauma. Those with mild forms bruise easily, suffer more nosebleeds, and bleed for longer periods after being cut. Those with more severe forms may bleed spontaneously or suffer from life-threatening blood loss after trauma. Bleeding may be controlled by augmenting the victim's blood with clotting components.

hemorrhoids: swelling of an anal vein, causing bleeding and itching around the anal area. Treated with high-fiber diet and suppositories.

high blood pressure: the higher the blood pressure the greater the risk of stroke and heart attack. Controlled by diet and drug therapy. Also known as hypertension.

high cholesterol: any cholesterol level over 200. Generally, the higher the number the greater the risk of developing heart and artery disease. Controlled by a low-fat diet and sometimes drugs.

Hodgkin's Disease: a chronic, progressive disease marked by enlargement of the lymph nodes, spleen and other lymphoid tissues. The disease is invariably fatal if untreated but can be cured, even in advanced stages, with treatment. It occurs most frequently in people 15 to 38, with another peak after age 50. Symptoms include swelling of the lymph nodes, fever, night sweats, fatigue, weight loss and intense itching. Treatment includes chemotherapy and radiation therapy.

Klinefelter's Syndrome: a genetic abnormality that appears in males but frequently goes unnoticed until puberty. Characteristics of the disorder include a small, immature penis and small, firm testicles, overgrown breasts, a lack of facial or chest hair, impotence, and deficient or no libido. The syndrome is also associated with mental retardation and various personality disorders. Some of the symptoms can be treated with hormone therapy.

leukemia: a malignant proliferation of leukocytes (white or colorless nucleated cells) in bone marrow, lymph tissue and blood.

The disease occurs in adults, but it is the most common form of cancer among children. Symptoms include high fever, abnormal bleeding, easy bruising, weakness, lassitude and pallor. Leukemia has a variable cure rate with treatment, but is always fatal without the proper type of treatment.

Lou Gehrig's Disease: a muscular atrophy disease usually occurring between the ages of 40 and 70 and often fatal within three to ten years. Symptoms include: muscle weakness, especially in the hands and forearms; difficulty in swallowing, breathing and chewing; and impaired speech. Formally known as amyotrophic lateral sclerosis or ALS.

malaria: an acute infectious disease transmitted to humans by mosquitos in tropical and subtropical areas of the world. If left untreated, it is fatal to about 10 percent of its victims. The infection has an incubation period of 12 to 30 days, after the completion of which patients suffer chills, fever and headache. During acute malarial attacks, patients typically suffer a cold stage with chills for one to two hours, a hot stage with fever soaring as high as 107° for three to four hours, and a wet stage with profuse sweating for two to four hours. The infection can be treated with chloroquine, although chloroquine-resistant strains of the infection are spreading rapidly throughout the world.

malignant melanoma: a deadly skin tumor that frequently metastasizes to other body parts. Early symptoms include a skin lesion or mole that enlarges, changes color, becomes sore or bleeds. A melanoma may appear red, white or blue over a brown background and have an irregular or notched margin. It may sometimes take on the appearance of a blackberry or remain in the appearance of a very large freckle with black nodules. The tumor must be surgically removed.

Marfan Syndrome: a genetic degenerative disorder involving the connecting tissue. Its hallmark characteristic is a lengthening of limb bones. Sufferers have notably longer legs, arms and fingers, with a tendency for a shorter-than-average torso. Other signs of the disorder include loose-jointedness, funnel breast, severe myopia (often with quivering of the iris with eye movement), cardiovascular complications and scoliosis.

migraine: severe, recurrent headache, with pain usually on one side of the head and often accompanied by nausea and visual disturbances.

oligodendroglioma: a brain tumor occurring most often in middle-aged women. Typical survival time is five years. Symptoms, depending on location of the growth, include hallucinations of memory, vision, smell and taste, grand mal seizures, behavior and personality changes, dizziness and flashing lights.

osteoarthritis: the most common form of arthritis, characterized by joint pain and stiffness, with onset in middle age and progressive worsening into old age. Relieved by various pain-relievers.

osteogenesis imperfecta: a genetic disease, occurring in infants and children, characterized by brittle bones and recurring fractures. Young children with the disorder typically have a bulging or triangle-shaped head, large eyes with blue scleras, and out-jutting ears. Other signs of the disorder include translucent skin and discolored, cavity-prone teeth. Sufferers typically fear walking because of the frequent fractures experienced.

osteoporosis: a metabolic bone disorder marked by a slowdown or deficiency in the production of new bone mass. The resulting decreased density produces bone porosity and fragility.

ovarian cancer: common form of cancer found in women between the ages of 40 and 65 and most often in women of the upper socioeconomic level. The disease progresses rapidly, making for a poorer prognosis than other cancers, with early symptoms including abdominal discomfort, urinary frequency, constipation and weight loss.

pituitary tumor: a tumor growth found most often in men and women between the ages of 30 and 40. Symptoms include headache (front of the head) blurring vision progressing to blindness, dizziness, personality changes or dementia, decreased pubic hair and libido, and decreased skin wrinkles. Prognosis is fair to good with tumor removal.

precocious puberty: premature development of puberty, sometimes passed on genetically, sometimes caused by pituitary or hypothalmic lesions, by testicular tumors, by infection or by juvenile hypothyroidism. Symptoms may appear at a very young age and include, in boys, a fully developed, adult-sized penis and testicles, pubic hair, beard and deep voice. Boys as young as age seven with precocious puberty have reportedly fathered children. Girls typically develop breasts and pubic hair and menstruate before age nine. Hormone treatment can help prevent or lessen some symptoms.

premenstrual syndrome (PMS): the fluid retention, bloating, irritability, depression and fatigue that sometimes precede a menstrual period, more pronounced in some women than others.

progeria: formally known as Hutchinson-Gilford Disease, a very rare disease characterized by profound premature aging. Children with the disease remain very small, develop wrinkled skin and gray hair, and die young.

prosopagnosia: the inability to identify faces, even familiar ones, as a result of brain disease or damage. Remarkably, sufferers often recognize faces as soon as they hear people speak.

prostate cancer: one of the most common forms of cancer among men after age 50. The disease can be treated if caught early, but symptoms rarely appear before advanced stages. The symptoms include difficulty in starting urination, dribbling, and urine retention.

rheumatoid arthritis: a chronic inflammatory disease affecting the joints and surrounding tissues. The disease strikes three times as many women as men, most frequently between the ages of 20 and 60. Its early symptoms include fatigue, anorexia, low-grade fever and weight loss. Later symptoms include painful, stiff joints that feel hot, especially after inactivity and upon rising in the morning. The fingers also become markedly gnarled or spindle-shaped. Aspirin and heat applications work best to treat the pain and stiffness, although surgery is sometimes necessary in severe cases.

Rocky Mountain spotted fever: a rash-producing illness transmitted by the bite of a tick. Symptoms include high fever, severe headache, and aching in the muscles, joints and bones. The sufferer's tongue is coated white and gradually turns brown with progression of fever, and a rash spreads over the entire body. The infection is fatal in about 5 percent of patients. Treatment includes a course of antibiotics.

sickle cell anemia: A congenital anemia caused by a defective hemoglobin molecule that produces rough, sickle-shaped red blood cells. The sickle-shaped cells offer protection against malaria but can impair circulation, causing fatigue, shortness of breath on exertion, and numerous other health problems. Most sufferers, primarily African-Americans, die by middle age.

squamous cell carcinoma: a malignant skin tumor having the potential to metastasize to other body parts unless treated promptly. It occurs most frequently in light-skinned people with a long history of extended sun exposure. The tumor most frequently appears on the face, ears or hands. Treatment includes surgical removal, radiation therapy, curettage or chemosurgery.

stroke: a sudden cutoff of blood to the brain caused by thrombosis, embolism or hemorrhage, producing serious and often irreversible brain damage, paralysis and aphasia. Risk factors include atherosclerosis, hypertension, arrhythmias, diabetes, lack of exercise and cigarette smoking.

Tay-Sachs Disease: a genetic enzyme deficiency marked by progressive deterioration of brain and motor function, usually causing death by age 5. Symptoms, appearing at three to six months, include lack of emotional response to stimuli and a progressive weakening of muscles. Deafness, seizures and paralysis usually occur by 18 months, followed by a vegetative state. The disorder is most commonly found in the children of Ashkenazic Jews.

tinnitus: permanent ringing or buzzing in the ears, most frequently caused by an inner ear disease such as Meniere's Disease.

ulcer: a lesion in the stomach or intestinal mucosal membrane, most commonly found in men between the ages of 20 and 50 and in chronic users of aspirin or alcohol. Symptoms include heartburn, indigestion, and pain when the stomach is empty. A warm, bubbling sensation at the back of the throat may also occur. An ulcer may be exacerbated by stress, but is thought to be caused by a microorganism infestation in the stomach.

uterine cancer: the most common form of gynecological cancer, usually affecting postmenopausal women aged 50 to 60. Bleeding and uterine enlargement are typical symptoms. Treatment is often effective, but includes complete hysterectomy.

vertigo: dizziness and loss of balance, often a sign of inner ear disease.

warts: ugly skin growths most frequently appearing on the hands.

Additional Diseases and Afflictions

abscess

Addison's disease

Alzheimer's

anemia

anthrax

arteriosclerosis

asbestiosis

athlete's foot

backache

beriberi

black lung

boil

botulism

bronchitis

bubonic plague
bunion
canker sore
carbuncle
caries (cavities)
carpal tunnel syndrome
car sickness (motion sickness)
chickenpox
chlamydia
cholera
chorea
chronic fatigue syndrome
cirrhosis of the liver
clubfoot
cold
colitis
congestive heart failure
conjunctivitis
crabs (crab lice)
crib death (sudden infant death syndrome)
Crohn's disease
croup
cystitis
dandruff
diabetes
diphtheria
dysentery
dyslexia
eczema
emphysema
encephalitis
endocarditis
Epstein-Barr syndrome

flu
food poisoning
gastritis
genital herpes
German measles
gingivitis
glaucoma
goiter
gonorrhea
gout
Graves' disease
hepatitis
herpes
hookworm
Huntington's chorea
impetigo
incontinence
influenza
Kaposi's sarcoma
laryngitis
Lassa fever
legionnaires' disease
leprosy
lockjaw (tetanus)
lung cancer
lupus
Lyme disease
lymphoma
measles
Meniere's syndrome (also Meniere's Disease)
meningitis
mononucleosis
multiple sclerosis

mumps
muscular dystrophy
myasthenia gravis
pancreatitis
Parkinson's disease
periodontal disease
pertussis
plague
pleurisy
pneumonia
psoriasis
rabies
radiation sickness
Reye's syndrome
rheumatic fever
rickets
rubella
scabies
scarlet fever
sciatica
scurvy
shingles
SIDS (sudden infant death syndrome)
sinusitis
smallpox
speech impediment
strep throat
swayback
syphilis
tapeworm
tennis elbow
tetanus
thrush

tonsillitis
trench mouth
trichinosis
tuberculosis (TB)
typhoid fever
typhus
vaginitis
varicose veins
whooping cough
yellow fever
(See *Eyes*, *Complexions*, chapter one)

HOBBIES AND SPORTS

Hobbies

amateur archeology
amateur astronomy
antique book collecting
antique bottle collecting
antique collecting
antique restoration
astrology
autograph collecting
barbershop quartet singing
baseball card collecting
beano
bingo
bird-watching
black arts
bread making
butterfly hunting
camping

cat breeding
ceramics
chess
classical music
coin collecting
comic books
crafts
crocheting
dancing
dog breeding
dowsing
flying
fly tying
fossil hunting
gambling
gardening
geology
gourmet cooking
greeting card writing
ham radio
hang gliding
horseback riding
horse breeding
hypnotism
ice cream making
inventing
juggling
kite flying
knitting
letter-to-the-editor writing
magic
mime
miniature railroading

music (piano playing, guitar, drumming, harp, etc.)
mystery writing
nature walks
old car restoration
old movies
painting
palm reading
panning for gold
parachuting
photography
poetry
poker games
pottery
quilting
raising livestock
reading (mysteries, romances, etc.)
rock hunting
screenplay writing
sculpting
singing
spelunking (cave exploring)
stock speculation
taxidermy
travel
tulip growing
whittling
wine tasting

Sports

archery
Australian rules football
auto racing

baseball
basketball
billiards
bobsledding
bodybuilding
bowling
boxing
broncobusting
bullfighting
canoeing
cricket
curling
diving
fencing
field hockey
fishing
fly-fishing
football
frisbee
golf
gymnastics
handball
hockey
hunting
jai alai
jogging
karate
kayaking
lacrosse
luge
marathon running
motorcycling
mountain biking

mountain climbing
ping pong
polo
racquetball
rock climbing
rodeo
roller skating
rugby
sailing
scuba and skin diving
skating (speed and figure)
skiing (cross-country and downhill)
ski jumping
skydiving
soccer
softball
squash
steeplechase
surfing
swimming
tennis
thoroughbred racing
volleyball
water skiing
windsurfing
wrestling
yacht racing

SOCIETIES AND ASSOCIATIONS

Abortion Federation, National
Actor's Equity Association
Act Up

Adirondack Mountain Club

Al-Anon

Alcoholics Anonymous

American Civil Liberties Union

American Indian Affairs, Association on

American Legion

American Mensa

Americans for Democratic Action

Amnesty International

AMVETS

Animals, Society for the Prevention of Cruelty to (ASPCA)

Anti-Vivisection Society, the American

Arts, National Endowment for the

Astronomical Society, American

Atheists, American

Audubon Society, National

Bar Association, American

Barber Shop Quartet Singing, Society for the Preservation and Encouragement of

Bible Society, American

Big Brothers/Big Sisters of America

Boys Clubs of America

Boy Scouts of America

Camp Fire, Inc.

Cancer Society, American

CARE, Inc.

Chamber of Commerce of the United States

Chess Federation, United States

Civil Air Patrol

Common Cause

Composers, Authors and Publishers, American Society of (ASCAP)

Concerned Scientists, Union of

Congress of Racial Equality (CORE)
Conscientious Objectors, Central Committee for
Country Music Association
Daughters of the American Revolution, National Society of
Daughters of the Confederacy, United
Defenders of Wildlife
Dowsers, Inc., The American Society of
Ducks Unlimited
Elks of the U.S.A., Benevolent and Protective Order of
English-Speaking Union of the United States
Entomological Society of America
Experimental Test Pilots, The Society of
Flying Saucer Clubs of America, Amalgamated
4-H Program
Friends of the Earth
Future Farmers of America
Gamblers Anonymous
Genealogical Society, National
Geographic Society, National
Girls Clubs of America
Girl Scouts of the U.S.A.
Graphoanalysis Society, International
Gray Panthers, National
Greenpeace
Handgun Control, Inc.
Horticultural Society, American
Humane Society of the United States
Indian Rights Association
Jaycees, The United States
Junior Achievement
Kennel Club, American
Kiwanis International
Knights of Columbus

Ku Klux Klan

League of Women Voters

Lions Club International

Masons, Ancient and Accepted Scottish Rite

Mayflower Descendants, General Society of

Meteorological Society, American

Moose, Loyal Order of

Mothers Against Drunk Driving (MADD)

Motion Picture Arts and Sciences, Academy of

National Association for the Advancement of Colored People (NAACP)

Nature Conservancy, The

Numismatic Association, American

Odd Fellows, Order of

Overeaters Anonymous

Parents Without Partners

Philatelic Society, American

Planetary Society, The

Planned Parenthood Federation of America

Press Club, National

Recording Arts and Sciences, National Academy of

Rifle Association, National (NRA)

Right to Life

Rotary International

Save the Redwoods League

Science Fiction Society, World

SCRABBLE Crossword Game Players

Screen Actors Guild

Shrine of North America (Shriners Hospitals)

Sierra Club

Sons of Italy in America, Order of

Sons of the American Revolution, National Society of the

Sports Car Club of America

Students Against Drunk Driving (SADD)
Theatre Guild
Toastmasters International
TOUGHLOVE
UFOs, National Investigations Committee on
Urban League, National
Veterans of Foreign Wars of the United States
War Resisters League
Whale Protection Fund
Wildlife Federation, National
Wildlife Fund, World
Women's Christian Temperance Union, National
World Future Society
YMCA
YWCA
Zero Population Growth

COLLEGE DEGREES

B.A.: Bachelor of Arts
baccalaureate: bachelor's degree
B.Ag.: Bachelor of Agriculture
B.A.M.: Bachelor of Applied Mathematics
B.Arch.: Bachelor of Architecture
B.B.A.: Bachelor of Business Administration
B.D.: Bachelor of Divinity
B.E.: Bachelor of Education
B.E.: Bachelor of Engineering
B.F.: Bachelor of Forestry
B.F.A.: Bachelor of Fine Arts
B.J.: Bachelor of Journalism

B.Litt.: Bachelor of Literature

B.L.S.: Bachelor of Liberal Studies

B.L.S.: Bachelor of Library Science

B.M.: Bachelor of Medicine

B.M.: Bachelor of Music

B.S.N.: Bachelor of Science in Nursing

B.S.: Bachelor of Science

C.E.: Civil Engineer

Ch.E.: Chemical Engineer

cum laude: graduating with honors

D.D.S.: Doctor of Dental Science

D.L.S.: Doctor of Library Science

D.M.D.: Doctor of Dental Medicine

D.M.S: Doctor of Medical Science

D.O.: Doctor of Osteopathy

D.S.W.: Doctor of Social Welfare

D.Th.: Doctor of Theology

D.V.M.: Doctor of Veterinary Medicine

Ed.D.: Doctor of Education

E.E.: Electrical Engineer

honorary degree: recognition of achievement, not schooling.

J.D.: Doctor of Laws

J.S.D.: Doctor of Juristic Science

M.A.: Master of Arts

magna cum laude: graduating with great honor or praise

M.B.A.: Master of Business Administration

M.C.S.: Master of Computer Science

M.D.: Doctor of Medicine

M.Div.: Master of Divinity

M.E.: Master of Engineering

M.Ed.: Master of Education.

M.F.A.: Master of Fine Arts

M.L.S.: Master of Library Science

M.M.: Master of Music

M.S.N.: Master of Science in Nursing

M.S.: Master of Science

M.S.W.: Master of Social Work

M.Th.: Master of Theology

O.D.: Doctor of Optometry

Ph.B.: Bachelor of Philosophy

Ph.D.: Doctor of Philosophy

S.B.: Bachelor of Science

Sc.D.: Doctor of Science

S.J.D.: Doctor of Judicial Science

S.Sc.D.: Doctor of Social Science

summa cum laude: graduating with highest honors

Th.D.: Doctor of Theology

Th.M.: Master of Theology

OCCUPATIONS INVENTORY

abortionist

accountant

actor/actress

acupuncturist

advertising sales

aerobics instructor

allergist

amusement park owner

amusement park ride operator

anesthesiologist

antique dealer

appliance repair
appraiser, real estate
architect
armored car driver
art gallery owner
artist, graphic
artist, painter
artist, sculptor
artist, sign
astrologist
astronomer
attorney, district
attorney/lawyer, criminal
attorney/lawyer, divorce
attorney/lawyer, personal injury
attorney/lawyer, probate
auctioneer
auditor, IRS
auto body repair
automobile salesman
bagel maker
bagger, grocery
baker
bank teller
barber
bar owner
bartender
baseball player, minor or major league
beauty salon owner/operator
bed and breakfast inn operator
boatbuilder
boat charter operator (fishing, whale-watching, etc.)
bookseller

boutique owner
bowling alley owner
boxer, professional
bridal shop owner
building contractor
busboy
bus driver
butcher
butler
cabdriver
cabinetmaker
cardiologist
carpenter
carpet/rug cleaner
cartographer
cartoonist
carwash attendant
cashier
caterer
chef/cook
chemist
chief executive officer (CEO) of Fortune 500 company
child-care worker
chimney sweeper
chiropractor
circus performer
city council member
city manager
clerk, store
clock maker/repair
coast guard personnel
comic
computer programmer

computer repair

congressman/woman

construction laborer

contractor, general construction

copywriter

coroner

cosmetologist

counselor, marriage

dance instructor

data processor

dating service operator

delicatessen operator

dental hygienist

dentist

dermatologist

detective

dishwasher

diver

dogcatcher/animal control officer

door-to-door sales (Avon, encyclopedias, etc.)

drilling and blasting specialist

drive-in theater owner

driver's ed. instructor

drug dealer

dry cleaner

editor, book

editor, magazine

editor, newspaper

electrician

embalmer

emergency medical technician (EMT)

engineer

farmer, dairy

farmer, grain and vegetable
farmer, poultry and livestock
farrier
fashion designer
fireman
fish and game warden
fisherman
fisherman, lobster
fisherman, shrimp
flight attendant
florist
football player, professional
funeral director
furrier
gastroenterologist
geologist
geophysicist
golfer, professional
grifter
guide, backwoods hunting
gunsmith
gynecologist
hairdresser
handyman
heavy equipment operator (bulldozer, backhoe, etc.)
hockey player, professional
homeless shelter operator
horse breeder/trainer
hypnotist
infertility specialist
insurance adjuster
insurance agent
interior decorator

inventor
janitor
jeweler
judge
junk dealer
justice of the peace
landlord
librarian
lifeguard
limousine driver
loanshark
lobbyist
locksmith
lumberjack
machinist
magician, professional
maid
marina owner/operator
mason
masseuse/masseur
mayor
mechanic, airplane
mechanic, auto
messenger, crosstown
meteorologist
midwife
military personnel
mime
minister
mortician
motel owner/operator
mover
movie director

movie producer
museum curator
musician, street
musician, studio
musician, touring
neurologist
newscaster/anchor
nuclear physicist
nurse, geriatric
nurse, in doctor's office
nurse, labor and delivery
nurse, pediatric
nurse practitioner
nurse, surgical
nutritionist
obstetrician
oncologist
ophthalmologist
optometrist
orthodontist
orthopedist
otolaryngologist (ear, nose and throat doctor)
painter
paleontologist
palm reader/psychic
panhandler
paperboy/girl
paralegal
paramedic
parapsychologist
paving contractor
PBX operator
pediatrician

pest control/exterminator
pet shop owner
pet sitter
photographer, calendar
photographer, family portrait
photographer, fashion
photographer, newspaper
photographer, wedding
physical therapist
physician, general practice
piano instructor
pilot
pizza shop owner
plastic surgeon
plumber
podiatrist
police chief
policeman/woman
pool hustler
postal worker
priest
printer
proctologist
professor
prostitute/escort service
psychiatrist
psychologist
psychotherapist
publicist
publisher
race car driver, professional
radio deejay
radio station owner

radio talk show host
railroad engineer
rancher
real estate agent
real estate broker
real estate developer
receptionist
recording studio engineer
reporter, newspaper
reporter, television news
restaurant owner
reviewer, book
reviewer, movie/theater
salesman/woman
school principal
seamstress
secretary
security guard
self defense instructor
senator
septic tank cleaner
sex therapist
ship captain
shoe repair
shoe shiner
shop/store owner
ski instructor
skywriter (advertising)
social scientist
social worker
sporting goods store owner
stockbroker
substance abuse counselor

surgeon
surgeon, brain
surgeon, heart
surrogate sex therapist
surveyor
sweeper, road
swimming pool designer
tailor
tattoo parlor operator
tavern owner
taxidermist
teacher, English
teacher, French
teacher, geography
teacher, history
teacher, home economics
teacher, industrial arts
teacher, Latin
teacher, math
teacher, physical education
teacher, science
teacher, Spanish
teacher, tutor
telephone operator
telephone sales/telemarketer
television and VCR repair
tennis player, professional
test pilot
trash collector
travel agent
tree surgeon
truckdriver
typist/word processor

urologist
veterinarian
waiter/waitress
warehouseman/forklift driver
waterbed dealer
wedding consultant
wedding shop owner
welder
window washer
wrecking contractor
writer, advertising
writer, gag
writer, greeting card
writer, novel
writer, screenplay
X-ray technician
yacht builder
yoga instructor
zookeeper
zoologist

3

Facial Expressions, Body and Vocal Language

ANGER

Angry Speech

grind out the words between clenched teeth
stammer with rage
spit out the words with contempt
spew out the words with malicious glee
mutter peevishly under one's breath
speak with grave deliberation
speak with brutal detachment
speak with bitter resentment
taunt
sputter
splutter
scream in exasperation
mock in a sniveling sing-song
sibilate

sniff

snort

speak in ragged bursts

speak in strangled tones

speak in a voice as cold as death

gibber

croak

clip one's words

maunder into one's chin

speak in stentorian bellows

jeer

hoot

speak in grudging tones

snap

hiss

fume

bark

boom

cry

growl

grumble

huff

pant

roar

shriek

thunder

wail

yammer

blurt

shout

Angry Tones of Voice

edge of impatience creeping into one's voice
strained
taut
rising hysterically
rising an octave
thick with insinuation
tinged with menace
carrying an edge of indignation
degenerating to a guttural rasp
bellowing ferociously
ascending to a murderous falsetto
growing husky/hoarse
growing frenzied
dripping with spite
brisk, business-like
cool, icy
She/He said . . .

acidly	gruffly	sarcastically
bitterly	haughtily	sardonically
bluntly	hotly	savagely
boldly	icily	self-righteously
brazenly	in a huff	sharply
caustically	incredulously	sourly
coldly	indignantly	spitefully
crudely	irately	stubbornly
defensively	maliciously	testily
fiercely	moodily	venomously
frigidly	ruthlessly	vociferously

Angry Glares And Stares

scorching look
look over piercingly
keep-your-mouth-shut look

eyes narrowing with contempt
fix with a level stare
glower
scowl
turn a cold eye on
look venomously
regard with cold speculation
withering stare
warning look
eyes seething
eyes blazing murderously
eyes sharpening
eyes smoldering
study critically
frigid stare
sneer
shoot daggers
give the once-over
monstrous glare
regard bitterly
look down one's nose
gawk incredulously
scrutinize with hauteur
snarl
fix with a smoldering eye
eyes scour one's face

Other Angry Facial Expressions

lips curling with disgust
spasm of irritation crossing one's face
face hardening
stony expression

face flushing with indignation
eyes bulging from their sockets
eyes rake the room
mouth quirks in annoyance
spasm of irritation crosses one's face
face turning red, then purple
mouth crimps in annoyance
face hot and pinched with resentment
mouth tightens into a stubborn line
face grows scarlet and swollen from shouting
veins in the neck standing out in livid ridges
crazed look
implacable expression
bridle at a rude remark
unyielding jaw
sticking out chin defiantly
looking about wildly
eyes raking the room
predatory expression
mouth contorted grotesquely
smiling maliciously
dark, smoldering look
face a dark mask
a rose of indignation forms on one's face
face lit with bitter triumph
smile wickedly
smile in defiance
teeth gritted
lips pursed with suppressed fury
face pinched tight
arrogantly impassive
rolling one's eyes
knitted brow

brow wrinkled in vexation

regard with arrogance

sneer inwardly

Angry Body Language

stalk out

storm out

stamp out

burst into a room

hurl oneself through the door

lunge at

slap smartly

wag a finger at

gesticulate furiously

slam fist into open hand

throw up hands in disgusted resignation

bunch fists

fists convulsing with suppressed rage

blood surging to fists

loathing welling like bile from one's belly

the breath coming raw in one's throat

vein throbbing at temple

nostrils flaring

heart hammering

stomach knotting

digging nails into palms

muscle twitching at one's jaw

a vein in one's neck pulsing and swelling dangerously

face growing hot

muscles tensing

stiffen at one's touch

shrink from one's touch

cringe at one's touch
adrenaline coursing through one's arteries
feel waves of disapproval from another
feel waves of impatience from another

ANXIETY/TENSION/NERVOUSNESS

Facial Expressions

spasm crosses one's face
lip twitches
blink excessively
clamp and unclamp teeth
grind teeth
gnash teeth
smile spastically
force smile
smile too much
eyes take on a hunted look
face grows pensive
eyes haunted by some inner anxiety
face pales
chew on one's lip
stress line forms on brow
furrowed brow
face grows haggard with worry
face tight, pinched

Body Language/Reactions

stomach knots
stomach clenches
stomach shrivels
stomach flutters

butterflies in stomach
wave of acid wells up from belly
stomach contracts to a tight ball
stomach contracts like a fist
swallow dryly
gulp
lick dry lips
clear throat excessively
swallow a lump in one's throat
drum fingers
fidget in one's seat
shift and reshift one's feet
leg pumps up and down like a piston
toes curl in one's shoes
hands balled into fists
dig nails into palms
wring hands
clasp and unclasp hands
bite nails
crack knuckles
pace
make a great business of searching for one's pen
babble
clam up
jangle change in one's pocket
sweat trickles down from armpits
beads of perspiration form on forehead
palms grow clammy
sudden stab of anxiety in one's gut

Voice

strained
constricted

tight
cracking
strangled
quavering
edged with tension
struggle to control quavering
rises an octave
grows shrill

FEAR AND PANIC

Facial Expressions

peer about wild-eyed
eyes dart maniacally, picking objects out of the gloom
eyes widen in alarm
eyes become saucers
stare saucer-eyed
watch with numbed horror
eyes take on a hunted look
eyes transfixed with horror
stare with fascinated horror
stare catatonically
face stricken
blood drains from one's face
face pales
face grows ashen
face grows chalky
face becomes a mask of terror
face etched in desperation
facial muscles twitch nervously

Body Language

the small hairs on the back of one's neck stir

the sensation of a spider crawling up one's back

a prickling sensation up one's spine

hackles rise

skin crawling

chill running up one's spine

arms blossoming with goosebumps

throat closing spastically

gulping spastically

gulp air furiously

swallow a lump in throat

swallow dryly

knot constricting one's throat

nostrils flare/dilate

gasp

breath quickens

breath comes raw in one's throat

heart flutters in one's chest

heart palpitations

heart pounds/hammers/beats/throbs/flip-flops

heart performs paroxysms in one's chest

heart pumps spastically

nauseating spurts of adrenaline course through one's veins

blood pounds in one's throat

pulse roars in one's ears

knees quake

trembling

shuddering

skin grows clammy

feel a cold fist closing over one's heart

sickening wave of terror welling up from one's belly

the sensation of a trapdoor suddenly opening in one's belly
stand rigid with terror
stand paralyzed
mind reels
feel strangely disembodied
feel strangely semi-present
feel dreamlike
go into shock
faint
lips form a mute *O*

Voice

becomes high and hysterical
breaks
screams
guttural scream
let out a strangled cry
shriek
voice explodes out of one
voice shrill with horror
cry out in a voice raw with terror
grows maniacal
degenerates to a childish whimper

SHOCK/SURPRISE/ASTONISHMENT

recoil in horror
reel with astonishment
blink with surprise
flinch
cringe
wince

blench
jump reflexively
fall backward
shoot upright in one's chair
bolt out of one's chair
give a start of surprise
eyes blink with incredulity
face glazes with shock
stand as if shot and waiting to fall
gawk in disbelief
jaw drops
gape pop-eyed
give a startled gasp
the breath catches in one's throat
gape in stunned silence
eyebrows shoot up in surprise
eyes widen with alarm
a sudden spurt of adrenaline coursing through one's veins
stand flabbergasted/stupefied/thunderstruck
feel a rush of heat to one's face
heart leaps/hammers/palpitates/throbs

PAIN

Facial Expressions

wince
grimace
grit teeth
clamp teeth
grind teeth
snarl of agony spreads over one's face
face contorted in agony

face contorted grotesquely
face twisted in pain
clamp eyes shut
eyes take on a wounded look
face growing drawn and pinched
face dark with pain
brows furrowed deeply
blench
face pales
blood drains from one's face
veins standing out in livid ridges along temple and throat
face turning scarlet and swollen
make a pained expression

Body Language/Reactions

writhe
thrash
convulse with pain
hands balled into tight fists
knuckles turning white
body stiffening in apprehension
doubled over in agony
squirming
cringing
recoiling in pain
body locking into fetal position
swallow lump in throat
gulp
flinch
shrink
tense up
steel oneself

eyes brim with tears
tears well up

Voice

moan
groan
wail
howl
bawl
grumble
snivel
whimper
cry out
cry
sob
voice explodes out of one in agony
scream
shriek
let out a strangled cry

SUSPICION

eyes narrowed with suspicion
a "you-don't-really-expect-me-to-believe-that" grin
regard quizzically
eye skeptically
raise one eyebrow in a questioning slant
a long, searching look
a slow, appraising glance
scrutinize one's features for clues
study acutely
look at asquint

weigh one's reaction with a critical squint
glance at surreptitiously
furtive look
peer out of the corner of one's eye
give a sidelong glance
eyes narrow speculatively
exchange questioning glances
probing eyes
regard curiously
give a look of uneasy puzzlement
a dubious expression
an ironic expression
enigmatic expression
eyes fill with dark portents
examine one's face owlishly
a look of suspicious bewilderment
troubled look
steeple one's fingers and assume a judicial expression

GUILT

eyes widen incredulously
blink at owlishly
shameless grin
sheepish grin
insipid grin
smile like a saint
angelic smile
pitiful look of appeal
toes curl in one's shoes
deepening hue of shame
blush
flush

like the proverbial cat that ate the canary
elaborately casual expression
incriminating look
eyes blinking with incredulity
features remarkably composed and angelic
eyes widening innocently
sniff with haughty denial
impervious to scrutiny
inappropriately serene
eye one another conspiratorially
gawk incredulously

ARROGANCE

Facial Expressions

peer down one's nose
sniff haughtily
regard with hauteur
regard with a lofty expression
raise one's eyebrows superciliously
roll one's eyes
puff up with self-importance
assume a posture of superiority
sneer
regard snootily
eyes narrow with disdain
eyes narrow with contempt
regard critically
look at as one would a pair of manure-stained boots
look at as one would a cockroach needing to be stepped on
turn one's nose up
turn a cold eye on

regard with snobbish horror
flash a superior grin

DISGUST AND NAUSEA

Facial Expressions

lip curls in disgust
eyes narrow with disgust
nose wrinkles up in disgust
nostrils contract reflexively
bridle (as with a sudden bad smell)
retch
shake one's head greenly
feel the bile rising up in one's throat
feel a trapdoor open in the floor of one's stomach
cheeks bloat suddenly, as if holding back vomit
peer down one's nose contemptuously

HAPPINESS

Facial Expressions

eyes dance
eyes sparkle
eyes shining with pleasure
eyes crinkle mirthfully
eyes moist with joy
eyes brimmed with joy
eyes glinting with pleasure
pupils dilated
face beaming
face radiant with good cheer

face brightening
smile broadly
smile jauntily
grin
face flushed with happiness
cheerful expression
look of delight
look of bliss
look of rapture

Body Language/Reactions

swelling with good cheer
heart soaring
heart leaping
feeling of being airborne
sensing tide of joy washing over one
reeling with unfettered joy
surge of elation
intoxication of the spirit
buoyant mood
unsinkable spirit
giddy with joy
sunny feeling in one's soul
feeling bubbly
feeling euphoric
feeling whole
dizzy with glee
energized
invigorated
perky
hearty
blithe
vivacious

SADNESS/GRIEF/DEPRESSION

Facial Expressions

face twisted in anguish
face a snarl of agony
wounded look in the eyes
features fallen
face pale
blood drains from one's face
look of mute appeal
face scarlet and swollen from crying
eyes bloodshot from crying
despairing look
etched with sorrow
lost expression
face drawn
downcast
long-faced
incurably sad
dark with pain
dark shadows around the eyes
glum
pouting
hang-dog expression
face a study of desolation
face ashen
stricken look
hunted eyes
eyes haunted by inner pain
pensive look
pouty lips
bottom lip curling

moue
pouting grimace

Body Language/Reactions

lump in one's throat
throat constricted
throat closing
stomach contracted to a tight ball
eyes transfixed with shock and grief
heart aching with nostalgia
body slumped/slouched/hunched
chin sunk dejectedly into chest
feeling of a cold fist closing over one's heart
feeling of a shriveled heart
heart wrung with pity
chest heavy
shake one's head in commiseration
spasms of nausea from grief
the bad news striking like hammer blows
bleak, wintry feeling
feeling of navigating through emotional minefield
grief growing like a cancer
feeling of a dark cloud overhead
dull, empty ache gnawing at one's soul
tug at one's heart
delirious with grief
eyes brim/mist over
body wracked with convulsions of grief

Voice

voice a lifeless monotone
voice wooden, distant

voice as cold as death
voice quavering
voice cracking
hitch in one's voice
voice becoming high and hysterical with grief
wail with grief
dissolve into tears
moan
weep
blubber
howl
groan
sob
snivel
whimper
whine
bawl

LOVE/AFFECTION/LUST

Facial Expressions

gaze at candidly
exchange predatory looks
eyes dark and smoldering
regard provocatively
exchange scorching looks
stare adoringly
regard with open fondness
beam fondly
look at with reverence
wink at salaciously
shoot a knowing wink

knowing leer
conspiratorial leer
pupils dilate
shoot flitting glances up and down another's body
stare at one another ravenously
look at one like a stalking panther
eyes range freely up and down one's body
smile roguishly
flirt demurely
smile nastily
smile suggestively
run one's tongue slowly over lips

Body Language/Reactions

face flushes
dissolve at one's touch
melt like butter in one's arms
hot wave sweeps into one's belly
heart thumps/throbs/pounds/hammers/flip-flops
ache with an inner longing
grow feverish with desire
set one's blood aflame
kiss softly/roughly/savagely/deeply
breath ragged with desire
toes curl in ecstasy
breathe words of desire
writhe in pleasure

DRINKING AND DRUNKENNESS

General Expressions and Body Language

sniff one's glass like a connoisseur
swish wine on one's tongue and assume a judicial expression

bridle violently at the searing sensation running down one's throat

smack one's lips

swig lustily

quaff

down

gulp

guzzle

chug-a-lug

take a long draw

toss off

swill

commune with the spirits

sit in a happy stupor

giddy with drink

drink companionably among the ribald shouts of customers at a pub

grow increasingly pot valiant (brave only when drunk)

sprawl out on the floor, anesthetized with alcohol

head feels like a bag of lead

grow drunker than a brewer's fart

drunk as a lord

three sheets to the wind

pickled

soused

smashed

inebriated

reel

carom off the walls

stagger

sway

lose one's sense of equilibrium

SMILES AND GRINS

affected: phony, pretentious, forced or improvised. *She affected a caring smile.*

alligator: broad and menacing.

angelic: saintly, but possibly tinged with or hiding guilt. *Her smile was angelic—like the proverbial cat that ate the canary.*

animated: lively, spirited.

arch: gay and mischievous. *She smiled archly.*

beaming: radiant. *He beamed at her.*

beatific: blissful.

bel air: graceful, poised. *His bel air smile put her at ease.*

brave: courageous or ironic. *She should have broken down and cried; instead she put her chin up and smiled bravely.*

broad: big.

c'est tout dire: a smile that says (you have said) all there is to say. *He flashed a c'est tout dire smile then turned to leave.*

Cheshire cat: broad; a smile so big that no other facial feature is noticed.

condescending: patronizing.

conspiratorial: a clandestine, between-you-and-me smile. *The two spies smiled at each other conspiratorially.*

coquettish: flirtatious, as to serve one's vanity. *The schoolgirl smiles at him coquettishly.*

coy: affecting innocence or bashfulness, like a coquette.

crafty: skillful, artful or deceptive; cunning.

cursory: superficial; performed rapidly. *The bank clerk smiled cursorily and took my deposit.*

curt: short, possibly to the point of rudeness or nastiness.

defiant: a smile of resistance, especially with the chin thrust forward.

demure: modest or affectedly modest.

dirty: lecherous; leering. *He flashed his dirty little grin.*

dreamy: abstracted, deep in reverie. *He smiled dreamily.*

en rapport: in sympathy or agreement with another.

facial tic: twitchy, spastic.

fanatical gleam: enthusiastic, manic. *He peered at the rare postage stamp with a fanatical gleam.*

faux bonhomme: affectedly or falsely good-natured; a smile that feigns cheerfulness or friendliness.

fleer: sneer; to smile derisively.

forced: improvised.

gleeful: merry.

gracious: kind and courteous.

grimace: a twisting or distorting of the facial features, usually to express pain, disgust or contempt; an ironic smile.

guarded: leery, wary. *He told her she was beautiful; she smiled back at him guardedly.*

imploring: a smile of begging or appeal; beseeching. *The little waif made an imploring half-smile.*

improvised: forced.

incredulous: skeptical; a you-don't-really-expect-me-to-believe-that grin.

incriminating: one that gives away one's guilt. *She tried to suppress an all too incriminating smile.*

insipid: lifeless, lacking emotion, excitement or zest.

involuntary: genuine.

inward: a smile in thought. *He sneered inwardly at the man.*

ironic: having a meaning opposite of what is expressed.

knowing: a smile of recognition of another's actions. *He flashed her a knowing smile as they moved toward the bedroom.*

leer: a salacious sidelong glance. Also expresses malicious triumph.

lopsided: crooked.

malicious delight: cruel, hurtful, spiteful.

mocking: mocking the smile of another to show contempt.

mute appeal: a smile that beseeches, asks for help. *She gave the cop a smile of mute appeal.*

nasty: salacious or wicked. *She smiled nastily.*

nervous: forced, spastic, twitchy. Also, smiling too much to hide nervousness.

obligatory: one that is expected but unnatural or forced, as from a tired salesclerk.

patronizing: condescending.

pinched: tight, nervous, self-conscious.

placating: one that appeases or makes concessions to the wrath of another.

polite: tactful, diplomatic.

pursed lips: closed-mouth smile.

sardonic: scornful, mocking.

sheepish: embarrassed, humiliated. *He smiled at her sheepishly and removed his hand from the cookie jar.*

simper: a silly, self-conscious, tight-lipped and affected smile.

smirk: a derisive smile that suggests smugness.

sneer: a scornful look characterized by raising one corner of the upper lip.

spastic: twitchy, nervous, forced.

superficial: the classic beauty contestant smile.

superior: haughty or maliciously victorious. *He flashed a superior grin.*

thin: forced, closed-mouthed. *He smiled thinly.*

triumphant: victorious.

vague: half-hearted.

wooden: stiff, half-hearted, emotionless.

wry: a twisted or distorted smile expressing distaste or displeasure.

LAUGHS

raspy chuckle
hoarse chuckle
wheezy chuckle
maniacal cackle
roar
squeal
snigger
snicker
bellow
snort
bitter snort
belly laugh
titter
gales of laughter
great gusts of ribald laughter
hoot
guffaw
horse laugh
convulse with glee
lascivious laugh
giggle
demure giggle
bubbly laughter
nasty laugh
menacing laugh
contemptuous laugh
howl
mocking laugh
nervous laugh
forced laugh
restrained

hysterical laugh
scream
jubilant shriek
devious laugh
crow
tee-hee
cachinnate
polite laugh
obligatory laugh
staccato laugh
nasal whine
double over with laughter
guffaw
sibilate
laugh like a hyena

WALKING, RUNNING AND MOVING

Awkward/Difficult Forms of Walking

dodder
falter
hobble
labor
limp
lumber
plod
shamble
shuffle
stagger
stumble
totter
traipse

trudge
squelch through the mud
slog through puddles
slosh through slush
lean into the wind
battle forward through the wind
sidle through a crowd
elbow/shoulder/jostle through a crowd
blunder in the dark
crab on all fours
lope down a hill
glissade down a hill
backpedal
blaze a trail
bushwack
forge ahead
strain under a heavy load
clamber up
scale a ledge
continue on doggedly
make one's way

Complex and Elaborate Walking Forms

pick one's way around
thread one's way
maneuver
navigate
negotiate
weave
wind
wedge
skirt

step nimbly around
take a circuitous path
circumambulate

Cautious, Sneaky Walking Forms

creep
edge away
inch one's way
slip away
slink away
steal away
shrink away in silence
skulk
prowl
withdraw
lurk
shadow
tip-toe

Casual Walking Forms

amble
mosey
pad
saunter
shuffle
shuffle sleepily
stroll
tread

Angry Walking Forms

stalk out
storm out

stamp out
stomp out
catapult into a room
bust into a room
hurl oneself through a door
swoop into a room

Humiliated Walking Forms

skulk off like a kicked dog
go slouching off
go cowering off
walk away with elaborate nonchalance
walk away with an elaborately casual manner

Sexy Walking Forms

walk with porteuse grace
pert wiggle
feline grace
slink
voluptuous sway
strut

Miscellaneous Walking Forms

portly waddle
military gait
goose-stepping
proud, stately carriage
bowlegged stride
loose-boned gait
willowy gait
mincing steps
retrace one's steps

swagger
wander aimlessly
meander
walk resolutely
venture forth
toddle

Group Walking Forms

parade
march
file out
surge
troop
swarm
flood
spill out into the hall
pile out of
be borne along by a crowd

Running

bolt
bound
charge
dart
dash
flee
hurry
hurtle along
hustle
light
lope
race

rush

scamper

scoot

scramble

scurry

scuttle

skedaddle

skitter

sprint

spring

tear off

trot

jog

bustle

beat feet

run laboriously

puff one's way up a hill

wheeze and snort one's way uphill

puff like a bellows

chest heaving laboriously

legs pistoning wildly

COMMON GESTURES

characteristic gesture: any gesture that is habitual or characteristic of a protagonist. *He ran his hand through his hair in a characteristic gesture.*

conspiratorial gesture: a "you and I share a secret" gesture; any subtle, clandestine gesture. *She shot him a conspiratorial wink. Johnson made a conspiratorial gesture with his elbow to show where the gun was hidden.*

cursory examination: more than a gesture, a quick and superficial "once-over," as when examining something of minor interest. *She considered her nails cursorily.*

desultory examination: also more than a gesture, a manner of looking at or passing abruptly and unmethodically from one thing to another. *He handled the artifacts in desultory fashion.*

disgusted gesture: any gesture that illustrates disgust or contempt. *He fanned the air with his hands in a show of disgust.*

dismissive gesture: any gesture that says, "you're dismissed, you may go now." *When the wine steward came back for the fifth time, Harris made an angry dismissive gesture.*

elaborate gesture: any gesture too elaborate or complicated to put into words. *With an elaborate gesture, Mary showed how the machine functioned.*

embracing gesture: a ponderous arm gesture, as if embracing a subject. *When he spoke, he embraced his subject with broad, sweeping gestures.*

emphatic gesture: any excited or emotionally-packed gesture. *"No, no! This way!" Aunt Mimi gestured emphatically.*

flourish: a gesture of mock showmanship, as when a magician produces something from thin air. *The pirate produced the map with a happy flourish.*

graphic gesture: any gesture that illustrates an obscenity. *The angry truck driver made a graphic gesture.*

helpless gesture: a gesture that says, "Hey, I'm helpless, what can I do?" *Mary kicked the flat tire and made a helpless gesture. When asked directions, Pete only shrugged and made a helpless gesture.*

pantomime: an acting out or miming. *Little Joey pantomimed to the alien what a piggyback ride was.*

peremptory gesture: a gesture meaning finality and no further argument. *Wiggins waved off all further questions with a peremptory gesture.*

placatory gesture: a gesture used in an attempt to appease or yield to someone's wrath. *Jonathan, facing an angry, suspicious wife, made a feeble, placatory gesture.*

proprietary gesture: a gesture or movement that illustrates ownership or, more to the point, a "give me that, it's mine!" gesture. *She grabbed the vase in a haughty, proprietary manner.*

theatrical gesture: any exaggerated gesture that an actor might make. *Martha made a theatrical gesture to showcase the new Univac 3000.*

vague gesture: any imprecise gesture, especially used to give directions. *When asked for directions, the janitor scowled and gestured vaguely down the hall.*

4

Dress

DRESSES

American Indian: a buckskin dress trimmed with fringe and beads. Also known as a Pocahontas dress.

baby doll: fashioned after doll clothes of the 1930s, a smock-like dress with a high neckline and a yoke.

backless: any dress with an open or low back.

blouson: a dress having a blouse-like top.

bouffant: a full or bell-shaped skirt, frequently pleated or ruffled, joined with a snug-fitting bodice. Also, any puffy dress.

bubble dress: a dress having a bubble-like skirt and fitted bodice, popular in the late 1950s.

burlap bag: a descriptive term for any frumpy, shapeless or unattractive dress.

bustle: a dress originating in the 1830s and revived to peak popularity in the 1870s and 1880s. It was typically a long, flowing dress characterized by a stuffed pad, or tier of gathered frills, protruding from the rump.

caftan: a long, robe-like dress with long sleeves and an embroidered neckline, a Near East design.

cardigan: a collarless, button-down dress of various lengths, similar in design to a cardigan sweater, popular in the 1960s.

chemise: a dress hanging straight from the shoulders with no waistline. Also known as a shift or sack dress.

cocktail dress: a short evening dress with a low neckline.

crinoline: a hoop skirt, most popular from the mid 1800s to the 1870s. Also, a dome-, funnel- or pyramid-shaped understructure made of hoops or whalebone to widen the dress or skirt. Also, a stiff horsehair fabric used to stiffen and line the skirt.

cutout: a fad dress of the 1960s, characterized by cutouts or holes around the midsection and arms.

dashiki: a long, straight-falling dress with bell-shaped sleeves and African-inspired ornamentation.

diamanté: a flashy evening dress covered with beads, sequins or paillettes (spangles), popular in the 1980s.

dirndl: a bell-shaped dress with a gathered waistline and a tight bodice, designed after dresses worn by Tyrolean peasants.

Empire dress: a dress characterized by a low neckline, a high waistline, and a straight, narrow skirt, originating during the first French Empire.

Ethiopian shirtdress: a shirt with Ethiopian-designed embroidery.

evening gown: any formal ball gown.

flapper: a dress characterized by its long top and short skirt, originating in the 1920s and revived in the 1960s.

granny dress: any old-fashioned dress, but particularly an ankle-length dress with a high neckline and long sleeves trimmed with ruffles.

Juliet: inspired by Shakespeare's Juliet, a high-waistline dress with puffed sleeve tops.

jumper: a sleeveless dress worn over a blouse.

kimono: a Japanese robe or dressing gown closed by a sash. Also, a wraparound dress designed in this fashion.

maternity dress: a dress providing additional room in the mid-section for the comfort of pregnant women.

maxi: an ankle-length dress popular from 1969 to 1971.

micromini: a very short dress just covering the buttocks, popular in the 1960s.

midi: a calf-length dress popular in the mid to late 1960s.

minidress: a very short dress originating in the 1960s and revived in the mid 1980s.

monk: inspired by a monk's attire, a dress characterized by a cowl-like neck, bell sleeves and a cord belt.

Mother Hubbard: a loose, shapeless dress.

muumuu: a long, loose-fitting Hawaiian dress with floral print.

peasant dress: an old-world dress characterized by a snug bodice, puffy sleeves, a drawstring neckline and a gathered skirt.

pinafore: a sleeveless apron-like garment worn as a dress or over a dress, originally worn by girls beginning in 1870.

polonaise: classic dress of the eighteenth century, characterized by a fitted bodice and an open overskirt pulled back to reveal a colorful underskirt.

potato sack: a descriptive term for any shapeless, frumpy or un-flattering dress.

sack: See chemise.

sailor: a dress characterized by its sailor suit collar, popular from 1890 to 1930.

sari: a Hindu wrap wound about the waist and draped over the shoulder.

sheath: a tight-fitting dress with snug skirt slit down the back to make walking easier.

shift: See chemise.

shirtdress: a button-down dress reminiscent of a man's shirt.

shirtwaist dress: a dress comprised of a button-down, shirt-like top and a full, straight skirt, popularly worn in the 1930s and 1940s and revived in the 1980s.

slip dress: a dress hanging straight down from the shoulders by straps, reminiscent of a slip.

slit dress: any dress slit on one side to reveal a leg.

strapless: a dress held in place around the bosom by shirring or boning.

sundress: a casual strapless or halter-style dress.

sweater dress: any knitted dress.

tent dress: a voluminous, often triangle-shaped dress with no waistline, originating in the 1960s.

toga: a classic Roman dress or draping gown worn with one shoulder left bare.

T-shirt dress: a casual dress having a T-shirt-like top.

tube dress: a long, snug-fitting dress similar to a sheath.

wrap: any dress or garment wrapped or wound around the body.

SKIRTS

bell skirt: any flaring skirt similar to a bell in shape.

bouffant: any full or puffy skirt.

bubble skirt: a puffy skirt, reminiscent of a bubble, popular in the 1950s. Also known as a tulip skirt.

bustle: any skirt with a bow, gathers or a stuffed pad used to plump out the rump, popularized in the 1800s.

crinoline: a hoop skirt, popularized in the 1800s. Also, the understructure used to expand this skirt.

culottes: a pantskirt or shorts cut broadly to appear as a skirt.

dance skirt: a short skirt worn over a leotard and tights.

dirndl: a full peasant skirt gathered at the waistline.

Empire skirt: a straight skirt characterised by its high waistline, originating in the 1800s and periodically revived.

gored: a skirt comprised of multiple flaring panels.

granny: an old-fashioned, ankle-length skirt with a ruffled hem.

handkerchief skirt: a skirt characterized by its hemline, which hangs down in points.

hip-hugger: a low-hipped belted skirt of the 1960s.

hoop skirt: a bell-, cone- or pyramid-shaped skirt popular in the 1800s. See crinonline.

kilt: a wraparound plaid skirt fastened with a safety pin.

maxi: an ankle-length skirt.

midi: a calf-length skirt.

mini: a very short skirt ending above the knee, popular in the 1960s and revived in the late 1980s.

peasant: any full, old-fashioned skirt, plain or embroidered.

peplum: a flounce or overskirt worn over a larger skirt.

prairie skirt: a calico skirt with a ruffled hem.

sarong: a wrap skirt, usually having a floral print.

sheath: a straight, very snug skirt with a slit in the back to make walking easier.

slit skirt: any skirt with a slit on one or both sides to reveal the legs.

square-dance skirt: a puffed-out skirt with a ruffled hem.

trumpet skirt: a skirt characterized by a flaring hemline, reminiscent of a trumpet's bell.

tulip skirt: See bubble skirt.

tutu: ballerina's very short skirt.

wrap: any skirt that wraps or winds around the body and is fastened with a pin, button or sash.

Examples of Dresses and Skirts

stretch mini

sequined mini

candy box frou frou
denim mini
a mini pouf
floral-print skirt
tiered taffeta skirt
slitted black leather mini
foulard skirt
pleated silk crepe skirt
checked skirt cinched with a wide belt
strapless dress
tablecloth-check dress
low-cut dress
sheer, silvery lace dress
bare-backed, hip-hugging dress with a plunging neckline
body tube
slinky dress
long, sheath-like black velvet evening gown
strapless lamé dress
country gingham dress
calico-print dress
halter dress
cotton pegnoir
rayon (waitress) dress
voluminous dress
polka-dotted slip dress
soft crepe de Chine dress
knit dress with cutout shoulders
cotton dress with a sweetheart neckline
long turtleneck dress
sumptuous velour evening dress
elegantly tailored dress

pleated broomstick skirt
black dress with bell sleeves
crisp, business-like suit

PANTS AND SHORTS

bell bottoms: jeans or other pants with large, flaring leg hems, popular in the 1960s and 1970s, and revived by a small faction in the 1990s.

Bermuda shorts: plaid or print knee-length shorts.

breaker: side-zippered pants with a contrasting inner lining.

buckskins: Indian leggings made of leather.

camouflage: brown and green military pants.

Capri: snug-fitting, calf-length pants with short slits at the sides of the hems.

cargo: pants characterized by a pair of bellows pockets in the back and another pair of patch pockets in the front.

chaps: cowboy's protective leather leggings, worn over pants.

chinos: men's khaki-colored sport pants.

choori-dars: pants fitting snugly at the thighs and rumpled below the knees, popular in the 1960s and again in the 1980s.

Clamdiggers: trade name for snug-fitting, calf-length pants.

continental: pants characterized by a fitted waistband and horizontal pockets, originating in the 1960s.

cords: corduroys.

corduroys: pants made of corduroy with vertical wales of various thicknesses.

crawlers: bib-overall pants for babies.

culottes: short, broad-legged pants giving the appearance of a skirt when worn.

cutoffs: shorts cut from full-length jeans or other pants.

deck pants: knee-length boat pants, from the 1950s and 1960s.

dhoti: Indian pants with gathered waistline and puffy legs narrowing to the ankles.

drawstring pants: any pants gathered at the waistline by a drawstring.

dungarees: denim pants.

fatigues: the work pants worn by members of the U.S. Army.

harem pants: puffy pants gathered at the waistline and ankles, popular in the 1960s.

hip-huggers: women's bell-bottom pants designed to ride low on the hips, popular in the 1960s.

hot pants: very short shorts worn by women in the late 1960s and early 1970s.

jockey pants: riding breeches with jodhpur-like legs tucked into riding boots.

jodhpurs: riding pants with broad thighs and narrow calves.

lederhosen: leather shorts held up by suspenders, worn in the Alps.

Levis: trade name for classic riveted jeans.

luau pants: calf-length, Hawaiian-print pants worn at luaus.

overalls: denim pants with a bib top supported by suspenders.

painter's: pants with loops on the legs, originally designed to hold brushes and later adopted for general fashion.

pedal pushers: woman's straight cut-pants with cuffs, popular bike-riding pants in the 1940s and 1950s, revived in the 1980s.

spandex: See stretch pants.

stirrup pants: any pants with straps or loops fitting around the instep of the feet.

stovepipe: any tight, straight-cut pants.

stretch pants: any stretchy, elastic pants, such as those made of spandex.

surfers: knee-length pants worn by surfers.

toreador: Spanish bullfighter's pants, fitting snugly below the knees.

SHIRTS AND TOPS

blouse: a woman's loose, button-down shirt.

body shirt: a tight-fitting shirt designed to hug the curves of the body, popular in the 1960s. Also, a woman's snug-fitting top with attached panties.

bustier: a sleeveless, strapless, snug-fitting, waist-length top worn as an undergarment by women. A similar top may sometimes be worn on the outside.

calypso shirt: a shirt tied in a knot in the front to expose the belly.

camise: any loose-fitting shirt or smock worn by women.

camisole: a snug, waist-length top, sometimes having straps, worn either as a lingerie item or as an outer garment by women.

camp shirt: a short-sleeved shirt with two breast pockets.

clerical: a black or gray shirt with a standing collar, worn by members of the clergy.

cowboy: a western-style button-down shirt, with or without pockets, sometimes worn with a string tie or a neckerchief.

C.P.O.: a light, wool navy blue shirt with patch pockets.

cutoff: a T-shirt or sweatshirt cut off at the midriff to reveal the belly.

dandy: any frilly shirt, especially with lace or ruffles running down the middle of the front and at the cuffs.

dashiki: a large pullover made with colorful African-print fabric.

diamanté: a woman's flashy top richly ornamented with sequins, beads or paillettes (spangles).

drawstring: a shirt that closes at the bottom hem by a drawstring to produce a bloused effect.

dress shirt: a traditional pressed shirt worn with necktie.

dueling: a slip-on shirt characterized by its large, puffy sleeves, worn by fencers.

epaulet: a button-down, long-sleeve shirt with epaulet tabs on the shoulders.

fiesta: a man's white cotton shirt embroidered down the front, popular in the 1960s.

flannel: any warm shirt made of flannel.

formal: a man's long-sleeved, button-down white shirt with pleated front and French cuffs.

halter top: a woman's backless top with front tied by strings around the neck.

Hawaiian: a brightly colored floral-print shirt. Also known as an aloha shirt.

hunting shirt: a bright red wool shirt worn by hunters in the woods for warmth and visibility.

jockey: a woman's brightly colored silk shirt, fashioned after the silks worn by jockeys, popular in the 1960s.

midriff: a woman's shirt cut or tied below the bustline to reveal the midriff.

Pendleton: trade name for a heavy, button-down, plaid wool shirt.

polo shirt: a short-sleeved shirt with three or four buttons running from the collar to the breast. Shirts frequently have a small breast pocket.

rugby shirt: a sport pullover characterized by its broad, horizontal stripes and white collar.

safari: a button-down shirt with four large pockets in front.

tank top: a sleeveless, low-necked lightweight shirt with shoulder straps, worn by basketball players and bodybuilders. Sometimes referred to as a muscle shirt.

tunic: a very long blouse, sometimes hanging to the knees and gathered at the waist.

turtleneck: a long-sleeved pullover with a high collar that is sometimes folded over.

western dress shirt: an embroidered cowboy shirt trimmed with fringe, leather or sequins.

SWEATERS

Aran Isle: originating in Ireland, a round or V-neck pullover with diamond patterns and raised cable knitting.

argyle: a sweater with classic diamond-shaped figures of various colors.

bolero: a very short sweater worn open with no buttons or zipper.

cardigan: the classic "Fred Rogers" sweater, a coatlike sweater with a crew neck and long sleeves.

cashmere: made from the hair of the cashmere goat, which is especially soft.

cowl-neck: a pullover with a rolled collar.

crewneck: a pullover with a round neck.

dolman: a pullover with batwing sleeves.

fanny sweater: a woman's coat sweater that is long enough to be pulled over the buttocks.

fisherman's: Irish sweater of water-repellent wool, noted for its bulkiness and natural color.

Icelandic: a hand-knit sweater of natural-colored wool, usually with decorative bands around the neck.

jacquard: a sweater decorated with geometric designs (or a deer) on the front or back.

letter: the classic high school letter sweater, originally worn by a school's sport team members.

shell: a sleeveless pullover.

tennis: a white, cable-knit pullover with long sleeves.

turtleneck: a pullover with a tall, folded-over collar that covers the neck.

JACKETS

Afghanistan: a lambskin jacket with fur fringe showing around the edges, popular in the 1960s.

anorak: a hooded sealskin jacket worn by Greenland Eskimos.

battle jacket: a World War II army jacket ending at the waist. Also known as an Eisenhower jacket.

blazer: a single-breasted suit jacket with patch pockets.

bolero: a very short sleeveless, collarless jacket similar to a vest, originally worn by bullfighters but sometimes worn by fashionable women.

bomber: frequently made of leather but sometimes nylon, a waist-length, zippered jacket with slot pockets and ribbed waistband. Also known as a flight jacket.

buckskin: a deerskin jacket, often trimmed with fringe.

bush jacket: See safari jacket.

dinner jacket: a tuxedo jacket without tails.

double-breasted jacket: a jacket having two rows of buttons and an overlapping closure.

Eton jacket: a black, waist-length jacket with wide lapels, worn open in front.

fishing parka: a hooded, waterproof jacket with a large, kangaroo pocket across the front.

golf jacket: a light, waist-length jacket made of nylon and closed with a zipper.

hacking jacket: a single-breasted suit jacket with rear vent, worn especially for horseback-riding events.

jean jacket: a denim jacket

jerkin: a waist-length, close-fitting, sleeveless jacket commonly worn in the sixteenth and seventeenth centuries.

lumber jacket: a waist-length, plaid wool jacket sometimes worn by lumberjacks.

mackinaw: a hip-length jacket made of heavy wool, usually in plaid or blanket-like designs.

Mandarin jacket: a Chinese-designed jacket with a standing band collar.

motorcycle jacket: a waist-length, black leather jacket, sometimes fastened to one side in front.

Nehru jacket: a lightweight Indian jacket characterized by its standing band collar, popular in the 1960s.

Norfolk jacket: a belted, hip-length tweed jacket with patch pockets and box pleats.

parka: a hooded, lined jacket for cold weather.

pea jacket: a hip-length, double-breasted navy blue jacket made of wool, a U.S. sailor's jacket. Also called a peacoat.

reefer: a short, double-breasted jacket similar to a peacoat.

safari jacket: also known as a bush jacket, a khaki-colored jacket with four large front pockets.

shearling: a sheepskin or lambskin jacket with wool showing around the neckline, cuffs and hem.

smoking jacket: a man's velvet jacket tied with a sash.

snorkel: a parka with a hood that zips up over the wearer's chin.

toreador: a woman's waist-length jacket with epaulet shoulders, reminiscent of jackets worn by bullfighters.

tuxedo: a tailless formal jacket, often black with satin lapels.

windbreaker: a lightweight nylon jacket worn to cut wind penetration.

COATS

balmacaan: a loose, tweed overcoat with raglan sleeves and turned-down collar.

chesterfield: a single- or double-breasted overcoat with a black velvet collar.

clutch: a woman's buttonless coat held or clutched together with the hands.

duffel coat: a short, hooded coat closed with toggles, originally worn by the British Navy in World War II.

duster: a woman's long, broad-shouldered coat with large pockets. Also a short, light housecoat.

greatcoat: any large overcoat.

Inverness: a long coat with a detachable cape.

maxi: an ankle-length coat popular in the 1970s.

midi: any calf-length coat.

pelerine: a woman's short cape, worn over a coat.

raccoon coat: a long, bulky coat made of raccoon fur, popular in the 1920s and revived in the 1960s.

raglan: a loose overcoat with sleeves that join seamlessly to the shoulders.

redingote: a woman's long, lightweight, straight-cut coat with buttons and patch pockets.

reefer: a thick, double-breasted coat, similar to a seaman's jacket.

stadium: a long, water-repellent coat with a drawstring hood and large pockets, a favorite at outdoor sporting events.

swallow-tailed coat: a formal, evening-wear coat with trailing, scissor-like tails in the back.

toggle coat: any coat closed by toggles instead of buttons or a zipper.

trench coat: a long overcoat or raincoat having several pockets and a belt.

UNDERGARMENTS AND NIGHTWEAR

baby doll: a woman's very short, sheer nightgown and panties set.

bikini underwear: skimpy underpants or panties cut high, but not as high as French cut panties.

bodystocking: a form-fitting, see-through, full-length stocking-like suit. Sometimes called a cat suit.

body suit: a torso-hugging suit ending around the crotch, sometimes having shoulder straps and sometimes not.

boxer shorts: baggy shorts worn mostly by men, but sometimes by women in a pajama set.

BVDs: men's underpants or jockey shorts.

camisole: a short negligee or top with a low neckline and spaghetti straps.

chemise: a woman's slip-like undergarment, sometimes made of silk.

corset: a tight-fitting breast-to-hip garment designed to give support and accent a woman's curves.

crotchless panties: panties designed with an opening in the crotch.

demi-cup bra: a partially cut bra that reveals the top of the breasts for maximum décolletage.

flannel pajamas: warm, heavy pajama pants and top made of flannel.

French cut panties: V-shaped panties cut high to bare the upper legs.

garter: an elastic band used to hold a stocking up at the thigh.

garter belt: a belt with suspended straps for holding up stockings.

girdle: a tight, fat-reducing, waist-to-thigh corset.

G-string: a very skimpy loincloth or crotch cover held on with cord around the back.

kimono: classic Japanese robe with broad sleeves, held shut with a sash.

lace-top thigh highs: thigh-length stockings topped with lacy bands.

loincloth: crotch-covering cloth reminiscent of Tarzan's attire.

long johns: warm, long underwear.

lounging pajamas: any stylish pajamas for lazing around the house.

merry widow: another name for a corset.

negligee: a woman's lacy nightdress, sometimes sheer.

nightdress: a long, soft, cotton dress.

nightgown: any long gown, sometimes made of satin and sometimes slit at the side to reveal one leg.

peekaboo bra: a bra with front openings to expose the nipples.

push-up bra: a bra that provides added support to sagging breasts.

satin pajamas: pants and tops of satin.

satin robe: a robe made of satin, often with a terrycloth lining.

sleepshirt: any long, soft shirt, frequently slit at the sides.

slip: a silky, chemise-like undergarment with shoulder straps.

teddy: a one-piece, slip-like undergarment, combining top with panties.

terrycloth robe: a warm robe made out of towel-like fabric.

thermal knit pajamas: thick, warm pajama pants and shirt.

T-shirt: a light, short-sleeved shirt worn by men or women.

union suit: one-piece long underwear combining top and bottom.

SHOES AND BOOTS

ballet slipper: a very soft, form-fitting dance shoe.

Bean boot: a calf-high boot with the bottom made of rubber and the top made of leather, an all-weather outdoor boot.

Beatle: pointy-toed, ankle-high boots made famous by the Beatles in the early 1960s.

boat: a canvas shoe having a non-slip rubber sole for work on a boat deck. Also known as deck shoes.

brogan: a heavy, ankle-high work shoe.

chain loafer: a moccasin-like shoe trimmed with metal links.

chukka: a rubber-soled, ankle-high boot lacing down the front.

cleats: athletic shoes with rubber or metal ground-gripping projections on the soles.

clodhoppers: any large or heavy shoes or boots worn by farmers.

clog: a wood- or cork-soled sandal-like shoe.

combat: a high, rugged, waterproof boot worn by military ground forces.

cowboy: a leather or tooled-leather high boot with pointed or square toes.

deck: See boat shoe.

dress shoes: any polished black or brown leather shoes.

espadrille: a rope-soled canvas shoe, sometimes lacing up around the ankles.

flats: casual, low-heeled shoes worn by women.

gaiter: an ankle-high shoe with elastic sides and no fasteners. Also, a leather or cloth legging extending over the shoe from the ankle to the instep or from the knee to the instep. Also known as a spat.

galoshes: waterproof boots pulled on over shoes and fastened with either a zipper or a buckle.

go go: calf-high white boots worn with miniskirts in the 1960s.

golf: a rubber-soled, oxford-style shoe with traction spikes.

granny: an old-fashioned high boot, usually black, laced up the front.

half-boot: an ankle-high boot.

Hessian: knee-high boots with tassels, worn by Hessian troops and introduced in England in the nineteenth century.

high-tops: sneakers with high ankles.

hiking boot: a sturdy, ankle-high boot with deep tread, worn for hiking and mountain climbing. Also known as a wafflestomper.

hip: thigh-high rubber boots made for wading in a stream when fishing.

hobnail: a heavy shoe or boot with short nails driven into the sole to prevent wear and slipping.

jackboot: a heavy, above-the-knee military boot originating in the seventeenth century.

jodhpur: a side-buckled, ankle-high boot worn for horseback riding.

loafer: a moccasin-like shoe. See chain loafer, penny loafer.

Mary Jane: a child's low-heeled shoe with a buckle strap and blunt toe.

Miranda pump: made famous by Carmen Miranda, a pump characterized by its high, flaring heel.

moccasin: a heelless, soft leather slip-on shoe ornamented with fringe and beads, originally worn by American Indians.

mukluk: an Eskimo boot made from the hide of walrus, seal or reindeer.

mule: a backless shoe or slipper worn by women.

open-toed: a shoe with a hole in the front to expose the toes, worn by women.

oxford: a low, solidly built shoe that laces over the instep and comes in a variety of styles.

pac boot: an insulated rubber or leather laced boot with a heavy tread, for cold weather wear.

penny loafer: a loafer having a strap with a slot over the instep. Wearers often place a penny or other coin in the slot for fashion.

platform: a shoe having a raised sole or platform, worn for fashion or to increase one's height.

police: a high black leather boot, as worn by motorcycle police.

pump: a woman's strapless, low-cut high-heel shoe.

Ruby Keeler: a low-heeled pump tied with a ribbon across the instep.

running shoe: an athletic shoe with arch and heel support designed for jogging and running.

saddle shoe: a light-colored oxford with a darker brown leather "saddle" extending over the middle.

safety shoe: a rugged work shoe having a steel or reinforced toe to help protect from injuries.

skimmer: a flat-heeled, low-cut pump.

slingback: a pump with an open back and a heel strap.

squaw bootie: an ankle-high boot made of buckskin and trimmed with fringe and beads.

stiletto heels: woman's pump with a very tall, narrow heel. Also known as spike heels.

stocking shoe: a slipper-like shoe permanently attached to a heavy stocking.

toe shoe: ballet shoe with wooden block in the toe.

tuxedo pump: a low-heeled pump with rounded toe.

waders: waterproof pants-like boots for fishing extending to the waist or higher and held up by suspenders.

wedgies: a wedge-heeled shoe worn by women.

Wellington: a rubber or leather boot for all-weather wear extending to the knee in front but slightly lower in back.

white bucks: white leather oxfords.

wing-tip: an oxford ornamented with lines of perforations extending along the sides.

Sandals

alpargata: South American and Spanish sandals with rope soles and canvas uppers around the heels.

clog: wood- or cork-soled sandals with straps or material covering the toes.

flip-flops: See zori.

Ganymede: classic Greek sandals with straps lacing up the calf.

geta: a Japanese sandal raised on wood blocks at the toe and heel.

gladiator: a Roman sandal with straps running around the foot to the ankle.

huarache: a Mexican, sling-backed leather thong with a flat heel.

platform: an open sandal raised on a high platform or sole.

thongs: flat leather sandals with straps separating the first and second toes.

zori: flat rubber sandals with straps separating the first and second toes. Also known as flip-flops.

CAPS AND HATS

Alpine: a felt hat with a peaked crown. Also known as a Tyrolean.

beanie: a brimless cap or skullcap formerly worn by kids and college freshmen.

bearskin: made famous by the guards at Buckingham Palace, a furry, high-domed hat with a chin strap.

bellhop: an old fashioned pillbox cap with a chin strap, originally worn by bellhops.

beret: a cap resembling a pancake; a wool or cloth tam.

boater: a straw hat with a flat, oval crown.

bobby: the classic English policeman's hat characterized by its high dome and narrow brim.

bowler: English term for a derby, a stiff felt hat with a round crown.

bubble beret: a puffed-out beret, often worn askew in the 1960s.

busby: originally worn by certain regiments of the British army, a tall fur hat ornamented with a drapery hanging from one side.

bush: an Australian cowboy hat with a brim turned up on one side.

calotte: a leather or suede brimless cap with a stem.

cartwheel: a wheel-like hat with a broad brim and low, round crown, worn by women.

chukka: a high-domed hat with a narrow brim, similar to an English policeman's hat, worn by polo players.

cloche: a soft, bell-shaped hat pulled down over the forehead, worn by women.

coolie: a parasol-like hat made of bamboo or straw, used as a sunscreen by the Chinese.

cossack: a tall fur hat worn by Russian men.

crusher: any soft felt hat that can be folded or crushed and stuffed in a pocket for travel.

Davy Crockett: the classic coonskin cap, comprised of raccoon fur and dangling tail, wildly popular with boys in the 1950s and early 1960s.

deerstalker: the famous Sherlock Holmes tweed cap characterized by ear flaps and a visor extending in front and back.

derby: American name for the English bowler.

Dutch boy: a wool cap with a visor and a soft, broad crown.

eight-point cap: the classic policeman's octagon cap.

engineer's: the railroad worker's blue and white striped cap with visor.

fatigue cap: an army cap similar in cut to the engineer's cap.

fedora: a felt hat with a turned-up brim and a crown creased down the middle from front to back.

fez: a red truncated cone with a black tassel hanging from the crown, worn by Turkish men.

French sailor: a large cotton tam with a pompon on the crown.

garrison cap: an olive- or khaki-colored dress cap worn by American soldiers in World War II. It was creased lengthwise and could easily be folded. Also called an overseas cap.

gaucho: a black felt hat with a chin strap, originally worn by South American cowboys but adopted for general fashion by women in the 1960s.

glengarry: worn by the Scottish Highland Military, a creased hat ornamented with a badge on the front and two black ribbons streaming from the back.

Greek fisherman's: a denim or wool cap with a braided visor, popular with boaters in the 1980s.

homburg: a felt hat with a creased crown and a rolled brim.

hunting cap: a bright orange or blaze orange cap worn for optimum visibility while hunting.

jockey cap: similar to a baseball cap but with a deeper crown.

Juliet: a woman's skullcap, ornamented with jewels, pearls and chains, and worn with evening wear or a wedding veil.

kepi: a visored cap with a flat, cylindrical crown, and sometimes a cloth havelock worn to protect the back of the neck from the sun, worn by members of the French Foreign Legion. Also known as a Legionnaire's cap.

leghorn: a yellow straw hat with a broad brim, worn by women.

matador: a hat with an embroidered velvet crown and two projections reminiscent of bull horns.

mortarboard: the tasselled, square-topped skullcap worn by graduating students.

mountie's: a broad-brimmed, high-crowned hat creased into four sections, worn by state police and the Royal Canadian Mounted Police.

newsboy: a visored cap with puffed-out crown, worn by newsboys in the 1900s and made famous by Jackie Coogan in the movies of the 1920s.

opera hat: a tall silk hat with a collapsible crown, similar to a top hat.

painter's cap: a visored cap with a round, flat-topped crown, worn by painters.

Panama: a straw hat.

pancake beret: a flat tam, sometimes worn askew by artists. Also known as a French beret.

picture hat: a broad-brimmed straw hat worn by women.

pillbox: a small, roundish, brimless hat worn either on the front, side or back of the head. A popular woman's fashion of the 1920s and occasionally revived.

planter's: a broad-brimmed straw hat with an indented crown.

porkpie: a man's snap-brim hat with a low, flat crown.

Puritan: the classic tall black hat with black band and silver buckle worn by men in the seventeenth century.

Rex Harrison: a wool, tweed, snap-brim hat popularized by Rex Harrison in *My Fair Lady*.

safari hat: a brimmed straw or fabric hat with a round, shallow crown.

Scottie: similar to a glengarry, a brimless hat with a creased crown and ribbons dangling from the back.

shako: a visored, high-domed hat with a feather cockade, worn by members of a marching band.

skullcap: any cap fitting snugly around the head, as a swimmer's cap.

snap-brim: any cap with an adjustable brim.

sombrero: Mexican straw or felt hat with a high crown and a broad, upturned brim.

sou'wester: a New England fisherman's hat, with a high-domed crown and a broad brim that is longest in the back.

Stetson: the classic American cowboy or ten gallon hat.

stocking cap: a knitted winter cap with a long tail and sometimes a pompon.

tam: the Scottish tam-o-shanter, a beret-like cap with a pompon or tassel in the center of the crown.

tarboosh: a brimless, truncated cone, similar to a fez, worn by Muslim men.

top hat: a tall, stovepipe-like hat with a narrow brim and a shiny finish.

tricorne: the classic three-pointed hat of the eighteenth century.

trooper: a lined leather cap with ear flaps, worn for warmth by mailmen, policemen and state troopers.

turban: a linen scarf or head wrapping wound around the head.

watch cap: a knitted cap with a turned-up cuff, originally worn for warmth by sailors on watch, now in widespread use in winter.

X cap: A baseball-like cap with an X on the front, named for Malcolm X.

yarmulke: the embroidered or crocheted skullcap worn by Orthodox Jewish men and, on religious occasions, by non-Orthodox Jewish men.

zucchetto: a skullcap worn by a pope (white), a cardinal (red), or a bishop (purple).

GLASSES AND SUNGLASSES

aviator: sunglasses with oversized lenses, reminiscent of the goggles worn by early airplane pilots.

Ben Franklins: glasses with small elliptical, octagonal or oblong lenses, worn on the middle of the nose.

bifocals: glasses having split lenses to improve both near and distant vision.

butterfly glasses: sunglasses with lenses shaped like butterfly wings.

clip-ons: sunglass lenses that clip on over regular glasses.

Courreges: wraparound, headband-shaped sunglasses having a narrow window of glass or plastic in the center.

granny: See Ben Franklins.

half-glasses: reading glasses with half-cut lenses; they allow the wearer to peer over the frame to focus on distant objects.

harlequin: designer glasses with diamond-shaped lenses.

horn-rimmed: glasses with dark or mottled brown frames.

John Lennon specs: the English, steel-rimmed health service glasses made famous by Beatle John Lennon.

mirrored lenses: sunglasses with one-way reflecting lenses.

monocle: a single lens placed in the eye when needed and hung from a ribbon around the neck when not in use.

old army surplus: heavy, plain dark brown or black glasses issued by the armed forces.

owl: oversized glasses with broad lenses.

pince-nez: frameless, circular-lens glasses that pinch in place over the bridge of the nose.

planos: faux glasses with dark frames to create a studious look, worn only for fashion.

tinted: glasses with lenses tinted yellow, gray or other colors. The color may deepen when exposed to sunlight.

tortoiseshell: mottled brown frames made from tortoise or faux tortoise.

wraparounds: wide, headband-like sunglasses that wrap around the front of the head.

FASHION STYLES

androgynous look: a clothing and hair style that combines male and female characteristics.

Annie Hall: inspired by the lead character in Woody Allen's hit movie of the 1970s, a largely uncoordinated style comprised of baggy pants and challis skirts.

Bonnie and Clyde look: for men, pinstripe gangster suits; for women, above-the-knees skirts and a beret worn at an angle.

Brooks Brothers: tailored, upper-class or business look, featuring Ivy League suits, button-down collars, trenchcoats, balmacaan coats and tailored skirts.

Carnaby: the famous "mod" look of the 1960s, originating on Carnaby Street in London. It included miniskirts, polka-dot shirts with oversized white collars, bell-bottom pants and newsboy caps.

dandy: a somewhat feminine style of the 1960s and early 1970s, featuring ruffles at the wrists and neck, worn by both sexes.

flapper look: originating in the 1920s and occasionally revived by style-conscious women, long-torso dresses decorated with beads and ropes of pearls, worn with short bob haircuts.

gaucho look: style characterized by calf-length pants, long-sleeved blouses, boleros and gaucho hats, modeled after clothes worn by Spanish cowboys, popular in the 1960s and 1970s.

Gibson Girl: late 1800s, early 1900s look, occasionally revived through the century; lace-trimmed blouses with leg-o-mutton sleeves, high choker collars, and gathered skirts, worn with pompadour hairstyles.

granny look: frumpy, old-fashioned, ankle-length dresses with ruffled necklines and hems.

grunge: young persons' look of the 1990s, characterized by baggy, old clothes with holes in them.

gypsy: a style characterized by full skirts, boleros, shawls, head scarves and hoop earrings.

hippie look: the classic 1960s and early 1970s counterculture look featuring long hair, sideburns, beards, tie-dye shirts, peace symbols, tank tops, ratty jeans, miniskirts and love beads.

inner city: 1990 black youth style characterized by baggy, over-sized jeans and shirts and baseball caps sometimes worn backwards.

kiltie: classic Scottish style, with plaid kilt skirts, knee socks and tam-o-shanter or glengarry caps.

military look: combat boots, camouflage pants, fatigues, buzz haircuts.

peasant look: full skirts, puffed sleeves, drawstring necklines and aprons, an old-world, European look.

prairie look: midwestern style featuring calico dresses with high necklines and long sleeves.

preppy look: upper-class, Ivy League look featuring polo shirts, cashmere sweaters, chinos or corduroys, oxfords, loafers and pumps.

punk look: radical teen style, originating in the 1980s, featuring bizarre haircuts (mohawks, spikes, shaved, dyed), torn clothes, black leather jackets, slitted skirts, chains and safety pins.

retro: any vintage look revived from the past.

western: cowboy dance-hall look, with tight jeans, cowboy shirts, string ties, Stetson hats and tooled-leather boots and belts.

SUITS

chalk-striped suit: any suit with stripes slightly broader than pin stripes.

double-breasted suit: a suit having overlapping closing and two rows of buttons.

leisure suit: a man's pastel, polyester suit, characterized by a shirt-like jacket worn without a tie, most often associated with the disco era of the 1970s.

pantsuit: woman's suit with pants instead of a matching skirt.

pin-striped suit: any suit having very narrow stripes.

scrubs: surgical gown or surgical clothing worn by doctors in the operating room.

three-piece suit: a business suit consisting of jacket, vest and pants.

tuxedo: a man's dress suit characterized by its jacket with satin lapels and pants with side stripes.

zoot suit: a man's suit with very baggy, high-waisted pants worn with a long coat, with padded shoulders.

5

Dialects and Foreign Speech

Using dialect is a superb way of characterizing a speaker's dialogue. However, most inexperienced writers tend to overdo the odd spellings and end up confusing and irritating readers. A widely agreed upon rule of thumb with dialect is "less is more"; that is, use odd spellings to show foreign pronunciation only as an occasional reminder of the speaker's accent. A better method is to simply drop in a foreign word every now and then, for example, a German speaker uttering "Nein," or a French speaker using the occasional "Oui." An Italian character yelling something about his "passaporto" is fine, but be forewarned: Try to construct entire sentences or phrases in foreign languages you aren't familiar with and you will most assuredly make egregious grammatical errors.

Some writers skirt this problem simply by announcing that the speaker has a foreign accent; they leave it to the reader's imagination to fill in the rest.

Following are a few examples of odd pronunciation spellings. But common foreign words are given more often. These words provide the simplest and least confusing method to characterize a foreign or other type of accent.

SOUTHERN (U.S.) ACCENT PRONUNCIATION GUIDE

afraid	fried
beer	bare
big	beg
bill	beyill
boil	bawl
can	kin
can't	caint
chair	cheer
Coca Cola	Co-Cola
crying	crine
dog	dawg
drink	drank
ears	airs
eggs	aigs
eyes	ahs
fence	faince
fire	far
foreigner	ferner
hour	are
get	git
going to be	gombee
green	grain
hair	har
lies	lahs
life	lahf
light	laht
mail	mile
man	main
morning	mo'nin
paper	piper
pen	payun
police	PO-lees
read	raid
school	skull
sour	sar
store	stow

tell ....tail
thing ....thang
yell..yale
you all ....yawl, y'all

BRITISH EXPRESSIONS AND PRONUNCIATIONS

The British and the Americans frequently have their own unique words and phrases to denote the same things. A few examples:

American	British
advertisement	advert
all talk, no action	all mouth and trousers
antenna	aerial
apartment	flat
automobile	motor car
baby carriage	pram
bad manners	bad form
bar	pub
candy	sweets
caught with one's pants down	caught with one's knickers in a twist
checkers (game)	draughts
crackerjack, ace	dab hand
crazy, stupid	daft, daft as a brush
dog-tired	shagged
drive	motor
drugstore/druggist	chemist
elevator	lift
emergency room	accident department
exactly right	bang on
fellow	chap
folk music	skiffle
foul up/screw up	balls up
french fries	chips
friend/pal	mate

frigging/fucking ....bloody, bleeding, blinking, blooming
gas...petrol
guy...fellow, chap, sod
hogwash! bullshit! ....rubbish! rot!
hood of car ....bonnet
horse of a different color........another pair of shoes
idiot/fool ....berk, birk
janitor ....caretaker
lawyer......................................barrister/solicitor
look like hell...........................look like dragged through a hedge backwards
mack, mister, buddy, bub.......love
mayonnaise ....salad cream
minister ....vicar
movie..cinema
muffler on a car ....silencer
nothing ....bugger all
policeman ....bobby
potato chip ....crisp
repair, fix.................................mend
rug rat (toddler).......................ankle-biter
schedule ....(pronounced) shed yool
screw-up...................................cock-up, ball-up
shit! damn it all ....bother! damn! blast! the deuce!
shy ....backward about coming forward
silly, flighty, screwy ....barmy
smart aleck..............................clever Dick
static ....atmospherics
store...shop
suspenders ....braces
swim...bathe
talk show..................................chat show
telephone booth ....call box
thread ....cotton
toilet, john...............................loo

trash bag	bin liner
truck	lorry
trunk of car	boot
unpleasant	beastly
vacation	holiday

Always drop the letter "h" when a Cockney (East End or lower-class London) character is speaking.

> "The kids 'aven't 'ad their breakfast yet."
> "Over 'ere, men."
> "Like bloody 'ell."
> " 'ow 'ard can it be?"

Also, change any "AY" sound in words to an "I" (EYE) sound.

Pronunciation

Lake	Like
Bake	Bike
Mate	Mite
Educate	Edyookite

" 'ow's your 'edache, mite?"

And change any "I" (EYE) sound to an "OI" (oil) sound.

Pronunciation

Ice	Ois
I	Oi
Right	Roit
Night	Noit

"Bloody well roit, mite."

With more upper-class British dialects, change "ah" sounds to "o" (dog, bog) sounds.

Pronunciation

Park	Pok
Father	Fother
Arm	Om

Change "a" sounds (man, tan, laugh) to "ah" sounds.

Pronunciation

Dance..dAHns
Nasty ....nAHsty
Ask ....AHsk
Laugh..lAHf

Change "oh" sounds (bone, home) to "eh-oo" sounds.

Pronunciation

Moan ....mEH-OOn
Bone ....bEH-OOn
Stone ....stEH-OOn

"Pok your mehootercaw and come in from this nahsty weather."

FRENCH VOCABULARY

airplane ....avion
airport..aéroport
alone..seul
and...et
angry..fâché
apple...pomme
automatic ....automatique
baby ....bébé
bad..mauvais
bag ....sac
bank..banque
bashful..timide
bath...bain
beach ....plage
beautiful ....beau
because.......................................parce que

bed	lit
bedroom	chambre à coucher
begin	commencer
below	dessous
blanket	couverture
blood	sang
boat	bateau
bomb	bombe
border	frontière
bottle	bouteille
boy	garçon
bread	pain
breakfast	déjeuner
bridge	pont
brother	frère
building	bâtiment
buy	acheter
call	appeler
car	voiture
careful	soigneux
cat	chat
chair	chaise
cheese	fromage
chicken	poulet
child	enfant
church	église
clock	horloge
clothing	vêtements
cloud	nuage
cockroach	cafard
coffee	café
cold	froid
come	venir
cost	coût
cup	tasse
danger	danger
dark	obscur
daughter	fille

day	jour
death	mort
dinner	dîner
dog	chien
door	porte
drive	conduire
drug	drogue
eat	manger
entrance	entrée
eye	oeil
eyeglasses	lunettes
factory	usine
fast	vite
fat	graisse
father	père
fire	feu
fly	mouche
food	nourriture
forbidden	défendu
free	libre
friend	ami
from	de
front	façade
garden	jardin
gasoline	essence
girl	jeune fille
go	aller
God	Dieu
good	bon
good-bye	au revoir (or) adieu
gun	arm de feu
hair	cheveux
hat	chapeau
help	aider
here	ici
highway	route
horse	cheval
house	maison

hungry ....affamé
ice cream ....glace
kitchen ....cuisine
late ....tard
light ....lumière
living room...........................salon
love..amour
mail ....poste
man..homme
map..carte
maybe ....peut-être
me...moi
meat.......................................viande
medicine ....médicament
milk ....lait
mistake ....erreur
money.....................................argent
moon ....lune
mother...................................mère
movie......................................cinéma
much ....beaucoup
name......................................nom
night ....nuit
no..non
open..ouvert
outside....................................dehors
pain ....douleur
pen..plume
physician................................médecin
please ....s'il vous plaît
potato ....pomme de terre
price ....prix
quiet ....tranquille
rain ....pluie
red ....rouge

river	fleuve
room	chambre
sad	triste
salt	sel
school	école
sea	mer
see	voir
see you later	à bientôt
sell	vendre
shave	raser
shirt	chemise
shoe	soulier
sick	malade
sky	ciel
sleep	dormier
small	petit
smoke	fumée
snow	neige
soap	savon
soldier	soldat
soup	potage
speak	parler
steal	voler
stop	arrêt
store	magasin
storm	orage
street	rue
summer	été
sun	soleil
supper	souper
sweet	doux
talk	parler
thanks	merci
the	le (or la or les)
there	là
thief	voleur
time	temps
today	aujourd'hui
toilet	cabinet

tomorrow...................................demain
towel...serviette
town ....ville
travel ....voyager
tree...arbre
understand ....comprendre
wait...attendre
waiter ....garçon
walk...promener
war..guerre
warm ....chaud
water..eau
where..où
who...qui
why...pourquoi
woman.......................................femme
work ....travail
wrong ....faux
yes ....oui
one..un
two...deux
three ....trois
four ....quatre
five..cinq
six ....six
seven ....sept
eight..huit
nine ....neuf
ten...dix

SPANISH VOCABULARY

accident....................................accidente
afternoon ....tarde
again ....otra vez
airplane ....aeroplano
airport......................................aeropuerto
alone..solo

ambassador ....embajador
angry.......................................enojado
apartment...............................piso
apple.......................................manzana
arrival ....erjercito
authority.................................autoridad
automatic ....automático
automóbile ....automóvil
baby ....nene
bad..malo
bag ....saco
bandage ....venda
bank..banco
bashful....................................tímido
bath...baño
battery ....pila
beach ....playa
beautiful ....hermoso
because....................................porque
bed...cama
bedroom ....dormitorio
beer..cerveza
blanket.....................................manta
blood ....sangre
boat..barco
bomb..bomba
book...libro
bottle ....botella
boy...muchacho
bread..pan
breakfast ....desayuno
building....................................edificio
business...................................negocio
buy...comprar
car..coche
careful ....cuidadoso
cash ....dinero contante
cat ....gato

caution .... cautela
cheese .... queso
chicken .... pollo
child .... niño
cigarette .... cigarillo
clothing .... ropa
cloud .... nube
coat .... chaqueta
cockroach .... cucaracha
coffee .... café
cold .... frío
come .... venir
courage .... coraje
cup .... taza
danger .... peligro
dark .... obscuro
day .... día
death .... muerte
dinner .... comida
direction .... dirección
dog .... perro
door .... puerta
dress .... vestido
drink .... beber
drive .... conducir
drug .... droga
eat .... comer
egg .... huevo
enemy .... enemigo
entrance .... entrada
exit .... salida
eyeglasses .... lentes
factory .... fábrica
far .... lejos
farm .... granja
fast .... de prisa
father .... padre
fire .... fuego

food	alimento
free	libre
friend	amigo
from	de
garden	jardín
gasoline	gasolina
girl	muchacha
give	dar
go	ir
God	Dios
good	bueno
good-bye	adiós
government	gobierno
gun	arma
he	él
help	ayudar
here	aquí
horse	caballo
hospital	hospital
house	casa
hungry	hambriento
ice cream	helado
information	información
kiss	beso
kitchen	cocina
knife	cuchillo
leave	dejar
life	vida
light	luz
living room	sala
love	amor
luggage	equipaje
mail	correo
man	hombre
map	mapa
masculinity	machismo
medicine	medicina
Miss	señorita (Mrs.—señora)

money......................................dinero
moon ....luna
morning..................................mañana
mother....................................madre
mountain................................montaña
movie......................................cinema
much ....mucho
name.......................................nombre
near...cerca
nervous...................................nervioso
newspaper..............................periódico
night ....noche
no...no
now...ahora
office..oficina
open...abierto
outside.....................................fuera
pain ....dolor
panic..pánico
passport...................................pasaporte
pay...pagar
pen...pluma
pharmacy ....farmacia
physician.................................médico
pig..cerdo
please ....por favor
post office...............................correos
potato ....patata
price ....precio
prison ....cárcel
quiet ....tranquilo
rain ....lluvia
restaurant ....restaurante
river...río
room ....cuarto
sad ....triste
safety ....seguridad
school ....escuela

sea	mar
see you later	hasta la vista (or) hasta luego
see you tomorrow	hasta mañana
sell	vender
shirt	camisa
shoe	zapato
sick	enfermo
sir	señor
sleep	dormir
small	pequeño
smoke	humo
snow	nieve
soap	jabón
soldier	soldado
soup	sopa
speak	hablar
station	estación
steal	robar
stop	parada
store	tienda
storm	tormenta
street	calle
student	estudiante
sun	sol
supper	cena
sweet	dulce
take	tomar
talk	hablar
television	televisión
thanks	gracias
there	allí
thief	ladrón
think	pensar
thirst	sed
ticket	billete
time	tiempo
tire	neumático

tired	cansado
today	hoy
toilet	retrete
tomorrow	mañana
towel	toalla
town	ciudad
train	tren
tree	árbol
trouble	molestia
truth	verdad
understand	comprender
urgent	urgente
village	aldea
violation	violación
wait	esperar
waiter	camarero
war	guerra
warm	caliente
wash	lavar
water	agua
weather	tiempo
wet	mojado
where	donde
who	quien
why	por qué
woman	mujer
work	trabajo
wrong	falso
yes	sí
one	uno
two	dos
three	tres
four	cuatro
five	cinco
six	seis
seven	siete

eight...ocho
nine ....nueve
ten...diez

ITALIAN VOCABULARY

accident....................................accidente
again ....ancora
airplane ....aeroplane
airport......................................aeroporto
alone..solo
ambassador ....ambasciatore
angry..adirato
apartment ....appartamento
apple..mela
army ....esercito
authority...................................autorità
automatic ....automatico
automobile ....automobile
baby ....bambino
bad...cattivo
bandage ....bendaggio
bank...banca
bashful.....................................timido
bath..bagno
beach ....spiaggia
beautiful ....bello
because.....................................perché
bed...letto
bedroom ....camera da letto
beef..manzo
blanket......................................coperta
blood ....sangue
boat..battello
bomb..bomba
book...libro
bottle ....bottiglia

boy	ragazzo
bread	pane
breakfast	colazione
building	edificio
business	commercio
buy	comprare
café	caffè
car	vagone
careful	cauto
cash	contante
cat	gatto
caution	cautela
chair	sedia
cheese	formaggio
chicken	pollo
child	bambino
cigarette	sigaretta
citizen	cittadino
clothing	vestiario
cloud	nuvola
coat	giacca
cockroach	scarafaggio
coffee	caffè
cold	freddo
consulate	consolato
correct	corretto
couch	divano
courage	coraggio
danger	pericolo
dark	oscuro
death	morte
dinner	pranzo
direction	direzione
disease	malattia
dog	cane
dress	abito
drive	andare
drug	droga

eat .... mangiare
enemy .... nemico
excuse .... scusa
expensive .... dispendioso
eyeglasses .... occhiali
factory .... fabbrica
far .... lontano
farm .... fattoria
father .... padre
fire .... fuoco
food .... alimento
forbidden .... vietato
friend .... amico
garden .... giardino
gasoline .... benzina
girl .... ragazza
go .... andare
God .... Dio
good .... buono
good-bye .... addio
government .... governo
gun .... arma
hat .... cappello
hate .... odiare
help .... aiutare
horse .... cavallo
hospital .... hospita
hotel .... albergo
house .... casa
hungry .... affamato
ice cream .... gelato
illegal .... illegale
information .... informazione
kiss .... bacio
kitchen .... cucina
legal .... legale
life .... vita
light .... luce

living room............................salotto
love..amore
luggage ....bagaglio
machine................................macchina
mail ....posta
man.......................................uomo
map.......................................mappa
market ....mercato
maybe...................................forse
meat......................................carne
medicine ....medicina
mistake.................................errore
money...................................denaro
mother..................................madre
movie....................................cinema
name.....................................nome
nervous................................nervoso
newspaper............................giornale
night ....notte
no..no
now..adesso
office.....................................ufficio
outside..................................fuori
pain ....dolore
panic.....................................panico
passport................................passaporto
pen..penna
pharmacy ....farmacia
physician..............................medico
pig...porco
please ....prego
potato ....patata
prison ....prigione
quiet ....quieto
rain ....pioggia
restaurant ....ristorante
river......................................fiume
room ....camera

sad ....triste
safety ....sicurezza
school ....scuola
sea...mare
see...vedere
shirt ....camicia
shoe ....scarpa
sick ....ammalato
sit..sedere
sleep ....dormire
smoke ....fumo
snow ....neve
sofa ....sofà
soldier ....soldato
soup...minestra
speak ....parlare
station...stazione
steal ....rubare
stop..fermata
store...magazzino
storm ....tempesta
street..via
student ....studente
sun...sole
supper ....cena
tea ....tè
teacher..insegnante
television......................................televisione
thanks...grazie
there ....là
thief ....ladro
thirst ....sete
ticket..biglietto
time ....tempo
tire ....pneumatico
tired ....stanco
today...oggi
toilet ....gabinetto

tomorrow	domani
train	treno
trouble	disturbo
understand	capire
urgent	urgente
violation	violazione
waiter	cameriere
war	guerra
warm	caldo
wash	lavare
water	acqua
weather	tempo
wet	bagnato
where	dove
who	chi
why	perché
woman	donna
work	lavoro
wrong	sbagliato
yes	sì
one	uno
two	due
three	tre
four	quattro
five	cinque
six	sei
seven	sette
eight	otto
nine	nove
ten	dieci

GERMAN VOCABULARY

accident	Unfall
airplane	Flugzeug
airport	Flugplatz
alone	allein

ambassador ....Gesandter
and..und
angry......................................böse
apartment ....Wohnung
apple......................................Apfel
army ....Armee
authority................................Behörde
automatic ....automatisch
automobile ....Automobil
baby ....Säugling
bad..schlecht
bandage ....Binde
bashful....................................schüchterr
bath..Bad
beach ....Strand
beautiful.................................schön
because...................................weil
bed..Bett
bedroom ....Schlafzimmer
beef...Rindfleisch
blood ....Blut
boat...Boot
bomb......................................Bombe
book..Buch
bottle ....Flasche
boy..Knabe
bread.......................................Brot
building...................................Gebäude
business...................................Geschäft
buy..kaufen
café ....Café
car...Wagen
careful ....vorsichtig
cash ....Bargeld
cat...Katze
caution ....Vorsicht
chair ....Stuhl
cheese......................................Käse

chicken ....Huhn
child ....Kind
cigarette................................Zigarette
clothing ....Kleidung
coat.......................................Mantel
cockroach ....Schabe
coffee ....Kaffee
cold.......................................kalt
consulate ....Konsulat
couch....................................Chaiselongue
danger...................................Gefahr
dark ....dunkel
day..Tag
death.....................................Tod
dinner....................................Mittagessen
disease..................................Krankheit
dog..Hund
dress ....Kleid
drive ....fahren
drug ....Arznei
dummy ....Dummkopf
eat...essen
enemy....................................Feind
excuse...................................Entschuldigung
exit..Ausgang
eyeglasses.............................Brille
factory ....Fabrik
far ....weit
farm ....Bauernhof
father ....Vater
fire ....Feuer
food ....Nahrung
forbidden...............................verboten
friend.....................................Freund
gasoline ....Benzin
girl ....Mädchen
give ....geben
go ....gehen

God ....Gott
good..gut
good-bye...................................auf Wiedersehen
government ....Regierung
gun...Waffe
hate..hassen
help ....helfen
horse..Pferd
hospital ....Krankenhaus
hotel ....Hotel
house ....Haus
hungry.....................................hungrig
ice cream ....Speiseeis
illegal.......................................ungesetzlich
information ....Auskunft
kiss ....Küss
late...spät
legal ....gesetzlich
life ....Leben
light ....Licht
living room..............................Wohnzimmer
love..Liebe
luggage ....Gepäck
machine....................................Maschine
man..Mensch
map..Landkarte
market ....Markt
meat...Fleisch
medicine ....Medizin
milk ....Milch
mistake ....Irrtum
moon ....Mond
mother.....................................Mutter
movie..Kino
name...Name
nervous....................................nervös
newspaper................................Zeitung
night ....Nacht

```
no.............................................nein
office........................................Büro
pain .........................................Schmerz
panic.........................................Schreck
passport.....................................Pass
pay...........................................zahlen
peace ........................................Frieden
pen...........................................Federhalter
pharmacy ....................................Apotheke
physician....................................Arzt
pig...........................................Schwein
please .......................................bitte
prison .......................................Gefängnis
quiet ........................................ruhig
radio ........................................Radio
rain .........................................Regen
restaurant ..................................Gasthaus
river ........................................Fluss
room ........................................Zimmer
sad ..........................................traurig
school .......................................Schule
sea...........................................Meer
see...........................................sehen
shirt ........................................Hemd
shoe .........................................Schuh
sick .........................................krank
small.........................................klein
smoke .......................................Rauch
snow ........................................Schnee
soap .........................................Seife
sofa .........................................Sofa
soldier ......................................Soldat
soup.........................................Suppe
station.......................................Bahnhof
stop.........................................Haltestelle
store.........................................Laden
storm .......................................Sturm
street........................................Strasse
```

student ....Schüler
sun..Sonne
supper ....Abendessen
table.......................................Tisch
talk...reden
teacher...................................Lehrer
television................................Fernsehen
thanks....................................danke
the..der (or das)
thief ....Dieb
thirst ....Durst
time ....Zeit
tire ....Reifen
tired ....müde
today......................................heute
toilet ....Abort
tomorrow...............................morgen
towel......................................Handtuch
town ....Stadt
train ....Zug
trouble ....Verdruss
understand ....verstehen
urgent ....dringend
violation ....Verlutzung
waiter ....Kellner
war...Krieg
wash ....waschen
water......................................Wasser
weather..................................Wetter
where.....................................wo
who..wer
why..warum
woman...................................Frau
work ....Arbeit
wrong ....falsch
yes ....ja
one...ein
two...zwei

three	drei
four	vier
five	funf
six	sechs
seven	sieben
eight	acht
nine	neun
ten	zehn

RUSSIAN VOCABULARY

airplane	samalyot
airport	aerodrom
alone	adin
ambassador	pasol
angry	zloy
apartment	kvartira
apple	yabloko
army	armiya
authority	nachalstvo
automatic	aftamaticheski
automobile	aftamabil
baby	rebyonak
bad	plakhoy
bandage	bandash
bath	kupanye
beach	plyash
beautiful	krasivi
bed	kravat
bedroom	spalnya
beef	gavyadina
beer	pivo
blanket	adealo
blood	krof
boat	lotka
bomb	bomba
book	kniga

bottle	butilka
boy	malchik
bread	khlep
breakfast	zaftrak
brother	brat
building	zdaniye
business	targovlya
butcher	myesnik
buy	kupit
café	kafye
car	pavoska
careful	astarozhni
cash	nalichniye
cat	koshka
caution	astarozhnost
chair	stul
cheese	sir
chicken	kuritsa
child	ditya
cigarette	papirosa
citizen	grazhdanin
clothing	adyezhda
cloud	oblako
coat	palto
cockroach	tarakan
coffee	kofe
cold	khalodni
come	prikhadit
correct	pravilni
courage	muzhestvo
cup	chashka
danger	apasnost
dark	tyomni
day	dyen
death	smyert
dinner	abyet
direction	napravlyeniye
disease	balyezn

dog...sabaka
dress ....platya
drink...pit
drive ....yekhat
drug ....lekarstvo
enemy.......................................vra
entrance...................................fkhot
exit...vikhot
expensive ....daragoy
eyeglasses...............................achki
factory ....zavod
far ....daleko
farm ....fyerma
father ....atyets
fire ....agon
food ....pishcha
forbidden.................................zapreshchenni
free...svabodni
friend.......................................druk
garden.....................................sat
gasoline ....benzine
girl ....dyevushka
God ....bokh
good...kharoshi
good-bye.................................do zvidaniya
government ....pravitelstvo
guest ....gost
gun...aruzhiye
hat...shlyapa
hate...nenavidet
he...on
help ....pomagat
here...zdyes
horse.......................................lozhat
hospital ....balnitsa
hotel ....gastinitsa
house ....dom
hungry ....galodni

ice cream ....marozhenoye
illegal.......................................nezakonni
information ....sprafka
kiss ....patselui
kitchen ....kukhnya
lake..ozero
late...pozno
leave ....ukhodit
legal ....zakonni
life ....zhisn
light ....svyet
living room...............................gastinaya
love..lyubof
luggage ....bagash
machine.....................................mashina
man...chilovyek
map...karta
market ....bazar
marriage ....brak
maybe.......................................mozhet bit
medicine ....lekarstvo
meet..fstryetit
milk ....malako
mistake ....ashipka
money..dyengi
moon ....luna
morning......................................utro
mother.......................................mat
mountain....................................gora
movie...kino
much ....mnogo
name..imya
near...blisko
nervous......................................nervni
never..nikagda
newspaper..................................gazyeta
night ....noch
no...nyet

now...tepyer
office..byuro
open..atkriti
outside.....................................na dvarye
panic..panika
passport..................................pasport
pay..platit
peace ....mir
pen..piro
pharmacy ....aptyeka
physician.................................vrach
pig...swinya
please ....pashalsta
potato ....kartofel
prison ....tyurma
quiet ....tikhi
radio ....radio
rain ....dozht
restaurant ....restaran
river ....reka
room ....komnata
run ....bezhat
sad ....pechalni
safety ....bezapasnost
sausage ....kalbasa
school.......................................shkola
sea..morye
see..vidit
shirt ....rubashka
sick ....balnoy
sit...sidyet
sleep ....spat
smoke ....dim
snow ....snyek
soap ....milo
sofa ....divan
soldier ....soldat
soup..sup

speak ....gavarit
station.....................................stantsiya
steal ....krast
stop...astanofka
store..lafka
storm ....burya
street.......................................ulitsa
student ....studyent
sun..sontse
supper ....uzhin
table..stol
talk...skazat
tea ....chay
teacher....................................uchitel
television................................televidyeniye
thanks.....................................spasibo
there ....tam
thief..vor
think ....dumat
thirst ....zhazhda
time ....vryemya
tire ....shina
tired ....ustali
today.......................................sivodnya
toilet ....ubornaya
tomorrow...............................zaftra
towel..palatyentse
town ....gorat
train ....poyist
tree...dyerevo
trouble ....gorye
understand ....panimat
urgent ....nastayatelni
violation ....narusheniye
wait..zhdat
waiter ....ofitsiant
war..voina
warm ....tyopli

water	vada
weather	pagoda
wet	mokri
where	gdye
who	khto
why	pochemu
woman	zhenshchina
work	rabota
wrong	nepravilni
yes	da
one	adin
two	dva
three	tri
four	chetirye
five	pyat
six	shest
seven	syem
eight	vosem
nine	dyevyat
ten	dye sit

6

Given Names and Surnames From Around the World

*T*here once was a Japanese man named Alister Wong. The trouble with Alister was he had a Scottish given name and a Chinese surname, and his surname was written last, which isn't done in China, but because Alister was born in Japan and raised in Brooklyn, nobody cared much. Alister's father was from Canton; his mother from the Firth of Forth.

As legitimate as Alister may be in the real world, be careful with such crossbreeding in fiction. Editors look for credible characters with credible names and backgrounds. Name all your Japanese characters Wu or Wing, and your Chinese characters Nakamura or Suzuki, and you give your ignorance away. Sure, it's OK to have a Dutch protagonist named Petit and a French villain named Van Horn: Just be sure your reader knows *you* know that your character is a curious hybrid.

If you've ever been wary of creating ethnic characters due to name phobia—or if you're unclear about whether Bruns is Dutch or German, if Alekos is a Greek boy or girl, or if Doloritas goes with Ivanov or Aguilar—the following inventory of foreign names is designed to provide thousands of credible mix and match possibilities to let you name with confidence.

ENGLISH

Surnames

Albert
Alcott
Alfred
Allbright
Allison
Ambrose
Ames
Attkins
Babbs
Bachelor
Baines
Barnes
Barrow
Barry
Bartlett
Beacham
Beadle
Beal
Bean
Beard
Beasley
Beck
Beckett
Biddle
Bidwell
Boxer
Brady
Bullard
Carpenter
Carswell
Cartwright
Chamberlain
Chambers
Chandler
Charles

Coldbath
Cook
Coppersmith
Darling
Dipple
Dobbin
Dodding
Doolittle
Drinkale
Drinkwater
Drinkwell
Dubber
Falconer
Farman
Gledhill
Godsafe
Greenacre
Halfpenny
Hamlin
Jagger
James
Jane
Jarvis
John
Jones
Jordan
Knight
Knighton
Merriday
Merryweather
Plummer
Rabbit
Radford
Radley
Ragget

Rainbird
Rainford
Seaborn
Seabright
Seagrave
Threader
Thurston
Tibbles
Tibbs
Watt
Weatherall
Weatherhead
Weatherly
Weathersby
Weaver
Webley
Weedon

Given Names

Male:

Adam	Clifford	Harrison
Alan	Clive	Harry
Albert	Colin	Henry
Alec	Corbin	Howard
Alfred	Craig	Hunter
Alistair	Cyril	Ian
Ambrose	Damien	Jack
Andrew	Daniel	James
Arthur	Darren	Jared
Austen	David	Jeffrey
Avery	Dean	Jeremy
Barclay	Devin	Joel
Barnaby	Donald	John
Barry	Dudley	Jonathan
Bart	Duncan	Joseph
Benjamin	Eaton	Keith
Bernard	Edmund	Kenneth
Bert	Edward	Kent
Blake	Elliot	Kevin
Brad	Elton	Lance
Bradley	Eric	Laurence
Brandon	Evan	Lee
Brent	Fletcher	Leonard
Brian	Frank	Leslie
Byron	Frederick	Lloyd
Cameron	Geoffrey	Mark
Carey	George	Martin
Cecil	Gerald	Matthew
Chad	Gordon	Maxwell
Charles	Graham	Miles
Chester	Gregory	Neil
Christian	Harley	Nicholas
Christopher	Harold	Nigel

Parry	Robert	Terry
Paul	Robin	Thomas
Perry	Roger	Timothy
Quentin	Scott	Walter
Reginald	Sidney	William
Richard	Stephen	Zachary

Female:

Agatha	Daphne	Jennifer
Agnes	Deborah	Jessica
Alice	Diana	Jill
Amanda	Donna	Joan
Amy	Doris	Julie
Andrea	Dorothy	Karen
Anne	Drew	Katherine
Ashley	Edith	Kim
Audrey	Elaine	Laura
Barbara	Eleanor	Leslie
Beatrice	Elizabeth	Linda
Becky	Ellen	Lindsay
Beth	Emily	Lisa
Beverly	Emma	Louise
Blythe	Erica	Lydia
Bonnie	Florence	Maggie
Brenda	Frances	Marcia
Brooke	Gail	Margaret
Candace	Georgia	Marilyn
Carol	Gladys	Mary
Carolyn	Hannah	Meredith
Catherine	Harriet	Michelle
Charlotte	Helen	Monica
Chloe	Hilary	Nancy
Christine	Holly	Natalie
Claire	Irene	Nicole
Constance	Jane	Olivia
Courtney	Janet	Pam
Cynthia	Janis	Patricia
Danielle	Jean	Paula

Peggy	Samantha	Tracy
Penelope	Sandra	Valerie
Priscilla	Sarah	Vanessa
Prudence	Sharon	Victoria
Rachel	Shirley	Vivian
Rebecca	Stacey	Wendy
Regina	Stephanie	Winifred
Rosemary	Susan	

SCOTTISH

Surnames

Abercombie	Farquhar	MacLeod
Abernathy	Finley	McClintock
Atherton	Forsyth	McCulloh
Balfour	Galloway	McCutcheon
Ballantine	Gladstone	McKean
Blackburn	Guthrie	McTammany
Blackwood	Haliburton	Oxnam
Breckenridge	Kilbride	Nesbitt
Clendenning	Kincaid	Newell
Cunningham	Kirkpatrick	Paisley
Dalrymple	Lithgow	Peebles
Dinwiddie	Livingston	Pringle
Drummond	Logan	Rutherford
Dryden	MacDonald	Sterling
Drysdale	MacDuff	Stocking
Dunbar	MacFerran	Stuart
Dunlap	MacGee	Urquart
Dunwoody	MacGuire	Weems

IRISH

Surnames

Bagot	Bailey	Bannister
Bagwell	Baldoon	Barlow

Beasley
Beatty
Begley
Begney
Biggins
Bigley
Boag
Boohan
Branigan
Cafferty
Carmichael
Casey
Cassidy
Clancy
Clegg
Corrigan
Coyne
Crumlish
Delaney

Devlin
Doonigan
Gallagher
Kilcooley
MacGillicuddy
Mackilcourse
MacMahon
Magilly
Manahan
McClure
Muldoon
Mulligan
Murphy
O'Brien
O'Connor
O'Dowd
O'Feeny
O'Finnegan
O'Flannery
O'Grady
O'Hanlan

O'Hara
O'Keefe
O'Leary
O'Neil
O'Reilly
O'Sullivan
Quigley
Quinn
Rafferty
Rooney
Scully
Shannon
Sheehy
Soolivan
Sullivan
Tenpenny
Wickham
Wiggins

SCOTTISH/IRISH GIVEN NAMES

Male:

Alister
Angus
Blair
Brandon
Brent
Brody
Busby
Callum
Cory
Craig
Darby
Darren

Desmond
Dillon
Donovan
Duane
Duncan
Erin
Erskine
Fergus
Gavin
Geordie
Glendon
Ian

Kean
Keenan
Keith
Kermit
Kevin
Lloyd
Neal
Orin
Paddy
Patrick
Quinn
Regan

Ronald	Sean	Shawn
Rory	Shane	Terrence
Scot	Shannon	Torrin

Female:

Aileen	Doreen	Lauri
Aili	Eileen	Mae
Annabel	Elissa	Maggy
Blair	Erin	Maureen
Brenna	Glyniss	Meara
Bridget	Guinevere	Morgan
Brittany	Gwendolyn	Regan
Carry	Jill	Rosaleen
Christel	Kate	Sheena
Cory	Kathleen	Sheila
Darcy	Kelly	Stacy
Deirdre	Kirstie	

FRENCH

Surnames

Arneau	Durand	Lerfervre
Beauchamp	Fonteneau	Leroy
Bellmonte	Fournier	Levesque
Bernard	Girard	Martin
Boudreau	Jacqueme	Moreau
Broussard	Jaillet	Petit
Cassell	Jantot	Rabaud
Comeaux	Jean	Rachet
Delacroix	Jeandeau	Racine
Descartes	Jeannet	Raine
Desjardins	Jehan	Raineau
Deveau	LaPierre	Raison
DeVille	Laurent	St. Clair
Dubois	Le Blanc	St. Cyr
Dumelle	Lemieux	Thibodeaux
Dupre	LeNoir	

Given Names

Male:

Adrian	Deon	Mathieu
Alain	Dominique	Maurice
Alban	Edouard	Noel
Ambroise	Emile	Pascal
Andre	Enric	Paul
Ansel	Fabrice	Philippe
Antoine	Fernand	Pierre
Arnaud	Francois	Regis
Beau	Gabriel	Remy
Bellamy	Gautier	Renaud
Benoit	Georges	Rene
Bernard	Gilbert	Robers
Blaise	Guy	Robert
Carol	Henri	Roland
Charlemagne	Herve	Royce
Charles	Hubert	Severin
Claude	Jacques	Seymour
Clemence	Jean	Silvain
Clement	Joel	Theron
Colbert	Laurence	Thibault
Damien	Leo	Valentin
Damon	Leon	Vincien
Dauphin	Louis	Yves
	Luc	
	Marion	

Female:

Adele	Angeline	Bernadette
Adeline	Annabelle	Blaire
Adrienne	Annee	Blanche
Alexandre	Annette	Brigitte
Alexis	Ariane	Camille
Alix	Aurelie	Carly
Amandine	Babette	Carol
Ami	Belle	Catherine

Cecil
Celeste
Celine
Cerise
Charlene
Charlotte
Cheri
Cheryl
Claire
Claudette
Clerisse
Colette
Coline
Constance
Danielle
Delphine
Denise
Desiree
Dominique
Elise
Emeraude

Emmanuelle
Estelle
Fabienne
Felice
Felicite
Gabrielle
Genevieve
Gisele
Isabelle
Janine
Jaqueline
Jeanne
Joelle
Josette
Kristell
Lorraine
Louise
Madeline
Marcie
Margot
Marie
Mariette
Maude

Michelle
Mimi
Monique
Natalie
Nicolette
Nina
Patricia
Paulette
Pauline
Raquel
Rose
Rosealine
Sabine
Sarah
Simone
Sophie
Sylvie
Veronique
Violette
Xavier
Yvette

GERMAN

Surnames

Bauer
Baumgartner
Braun
Bruner
Buchler
Burger
Danziger
Dreyfuss
Eisenberg
Eisenstadt

Elser
Fischer
Friedlander
Funck
Gerber
Groner
Hassel
Heller
Hoffman
Jager

Jahne
Kauffman
Kesler
Klug
Knef
Kraft
Kramer
Krause
Kruger
Kubek

Lahr	Schneider	Wagner
Lang	Schoenfield	Wald
Lauterbach	Schroder	Wedekind
Manheimer	Schuster	Weil
Metzger	Schutz	Weinberg
Moser	Schwab	Weiner
Muller	Sholtz	Weinmann
Myers	Shultz	Weiss
Neumann	Spengler	Wendorf
Oberlin	Stauffer	Wolff
Rademaker	Steinbach	Zimmerman
Richter	Steinhaus	Zinzendorf
Schaffer	Stumpf	
Schmidt	Vogel	

Given Names

Male:

Adelbert	Emil	Humfried
Albern	Ernst	Jan
Alvin	Faber	Jens
Anton	Franz	Jorg
Armin	Friedhelm	Jorn
Arndt	Friedrich	Julian
Arnold	Fritz	Karl
Berg	Gerhard	Kasper
Bernhard	Gerland	Klauss
Brendan	Gilbert	Klemens
Bruns	Gottfried	Kurt
Christian	Gunther	Leopold
Claas	Gustav	Ludwig
Conrad	Hamlin	Manfred
Daniel	Hans	Markus
Der	Hartwig	Mathias
Dieter	Heinrich	Max
Dietrich	Heinz	Meinhard
Eberhard	Helmut	Michael
Eduard	Hendrik	Nikolas

Oliver
Otto
Paul
Peter
Robert
Rolfe

Sander
Sebastian
Siegmund
Sigfrid
Stefan
Tobias

Ullric
Walden
Wilfred
Wilhelm
Wolf
Wolfgang

Female:

Ada
Adelheid
Andrea
Anna
Antje
Asta
Astrid
Berina
Berta
Bertha
Betti
Brita
Christa
Christiane
Claudia
Dagmar
Daniela
Domino
Elga
Elke
Else
Emma
Erika
Eva
Felda
Franziska
Frederike
Frida
Fritze

Gerda
Greta
Gretchen
Gretel
Hedda
Heidi
Helga
Herta
Hilda
Hildegarde
Inga
Ingrid
Jennifer
Julia
Karla
Karlotta
Katarina
Katharina
Katja
Katrina
Lotti
Magda
Marlene
Martina
Minchen
Mitzi
Monika
Nadine
Nastasia

Olga
Patricia
Petra
Runa
Sophie
Stefanie
Tamara
Ulla
Ursula
Valerie
Vera
Wilhelmina
Winnifred

JEWISH

Surnames

Aaron	Goldberg	Perlmutter
Abraham	Goldenstein	Rosen
Abramowicz	Greenbaum	Rosenbach
Abrams	Israel	Rosenbaum
Benjamin	Jacobs	Rosenberg
Bernstein	Kahn	Rosenblatt
Cohen	Kohn	Rosenblum
Dayan	Levine	Rosenkranz
Engel	Levinsky	Shapiro
Feinstein	Levinson	Silverstein
Finkelstein	Levy	Simon
Garfinkel	Lowenthal	Singer
Glick	Moscowitz	Solomon
Gold	Perlman	

DUTCH

Surnames

Bleecker	Hoek	Vanderbilt
Breitenbach	Huygens	Vandermeer
Brower	Kloppman	Van Dyke
Conklin	Mulder	Van Gelder
Cortlandt	Oberlander	Van Hoek
De Boer	Provoost	Van Hoorn
De Groot	Roosevelt	Van Ostrand
De Jong	Rutger	Van Pelt
Detweiler	Smit	Van Rensselaer
DeVries	Snider	Voorhees
Dykstra	Stuyvesant	Wannamaker
Frelinghuyens	Tappan	Wynkoop
Geis	Van Buren	Zeller
Haag	Van Camp	
Hartig	Van Cleave	

Given Names

Male:

Aart
Adriaen
Alarik
Andre
Ansgar
Barend
Bart
Ben
Berg
Bram
Carel
Carolus
Christian
Claus
Dane
Dirk
Erik

Fritz
George
Gijs
Gilpin
Gregor
Gunnar
Hans
Henrik
Jan
Jantje
Johan
Joris
Jules
Kasper
Kees
Klaas
Koenraad

Kris
Martijn
Matheu
Nicolaus
Niklaas
Otto
Paul
Peter
Pieter
Pippin
Rob
Schuyler
Valentijn
Van
Victor
Willem

Female:

Adele
Aleen
Amelia
Angelique
Anke
Annie
Beatrix
Betje
Brigitta
Catharina
Dacie
Danielle
Doortje
Edda
Elizabeth
Elsje
Francisca

Freda
Gijs
Gladys
Gustha
Janita
Jansje
Jetje
Jose
Kaatje
Katrien
Ketty
Letje
Lydie
Magdalena
Maryk
Pia
Sanne

Sonja
Sophia
Tryn
Velda
Wilhelmina
Wilna

SPANISH

Surnames

Aguilar	Gomez	Perez
Alvarez	Gonzales	Rabadan
Benitez	Hernandez	Ramos
Blanco	Jaen	Rivera
Cardoza	Jara	Rodriguez
Castello	Leon	Salazar
Cepeda	Lopez	Salinas
Cortez	Martinez	Sanchez
De la Fuente	Mendoza	Santiago
De los Puentes	Mercado	Santos
Diaz	Miranda	Sousa
Escobar	Molina	Torres
Espinoza	Montoya	Valdez
Estrada	Morales	Vargas
Franco	Nogales	Xavier
Garcia	Ortiz	

Given Names

Male:

Adriano	Cipriano	Ferdinand
Alberto	Ciro	Fernando
Alejandro	Clemente	Fidel
Alfredo	Colon	Filipo
Alonso	Damian	Flavio
Antonio	Delmar	Francisco
Armando	Diego	Galeno
Arturo	Domingo	Gaspar
Aurelio	Edmundo	Geraldo
Berto	Eduardo	Gerardo
Bonifacio	Emilio	Hernando
Carlos	Enrique	Humberto
Cesar	Esteban	Ibanez
Che	Eugenio	Ignacio
Chico	Felipe	Jacinto

Javier
Jesus
Jose
Juan
Juanes
Julian
Lazaro
Lorenzo
Luis
Manuel
Miguel
Orlando

Pablo
Paco
Pancho
Paquito
Pedro
Pepe
Pepito
Ponce
Rafael
Raimundo
Ramon
Ricardo

Rico
Roberto
Ruben
Salvador
Santiago
Santos
Segundo
Serafin
Tito
Vito
Yanez
Xavier

Female:

Adelina
Adriana
Alicia
Alita
Amata
Angelina
Anica
Anna
Aurelia
Beatriz
Belia
Belinda
Belita
Bonita
Brigida
Candida
Carlotta
Carmen
Charo
Cipriania
Conchita
Corazon
Cristina
Dela

Dolores
Doloritas
Dulce
Elena
Elisa
Elsa
Engracia
Esperanza
Estrella
Eva
Evelina
Evita
Felisa
Florencia
Francisca
Guadalupe
Ines
Isabel
Jacinta
Jauna
Jaunita
Joyita
Lela
Liana

Lola
Lolita
Lucita
Luisa
Manuela
Margarita
Maria
Marisa
Marita
Mercedes
Milagros
Mirabella
Olivia
Paloma
Paulita
Pepita
Pia
Pilar
Pureza
Ramona
Rita
Rosa
Rosalia
Rosalinda

Rosita
Sara

Serafina
Sofia

Teresa
Violeta

GREEK

Surnames

Anagnos
Anastos
Andros
Antanopoulos
Argos
Demopoulos
Demos
Frangos
Georgeakopoulos
Gianakis

Hondros
Karadimos
Karagiannis
Konstantopoulos
Kontos
Kotsos
Mackopoulos
Marangopoulos
Mikos
Nicopoulos

Panos
Papagiannopoulos
Papandreau
Pappadopoulos
Pappas
Pavlatos
Stephanos
Theodoropoulos
Vasilakis

Given Names

Male:

Alekos
Alexander
Alexios
Altair
Anatolios
Andonios
Andreas
Andrew
Apollo
Apostolos
Aristeides
Artemas
Athanasios
Baruch
Basil
Carolos
Christian

Christos
Constantine
Constantinos
Cosmo
Cyrus
Damian
Demetrios
Dinos
Dion
Emmanuel
Ennis
Feodor
George
Ignatios
Iorgos
John
Klemenis

Kostas
Kristo
Kyros
Lucian
Makarios
Makis
Markos
Maximos
Michael
Nicholas
Nikolos
Panagiotis
Pericles
Petros
Romanos
Sergios
Silvanos

Spyros
Stavros
Stefanos
Takis

Thanos
Thomas
Titos
Tonis

Yannis
Zeno

Female:

Agalia
Agathi
Aleka
Angela
Anna
Antonia
Arete
Aretha
Artemisia
Aspasia
Athena
Calida
Candace
Cassandra
Cela
Celena
Chloe
Clio
Cloris
Damara

Delia
Dora
Eleni
Esther
Euphemia
Evangelia
Evangeline
Georgia
Helena
Helene
Irene
Ismini
Kairos
Kalliope
Katherine
Katina
Konstantina
Lana
Lena
Lia

Maria
Niki
Nitsa
Panagiota
Rena
Rhoda
Selenia
Sofi
Sofia
Sonia
Stacia
Stefania
Tena
Teresa
Thea
Theodora
Vanessa
Zoe

ITALIAN

Surnames

Albano
Amato
Antonelli
Basso
Benedetto
Bianco

Bolino
Bonelli
Bono
Calderone
Campo
Caruso

Chiapetta
Ciccone
Colombo
Como
Copello
Cumo

De Benedictis
De Giovanni
De Santis
Ferrara
Fiore
Fosco
Galliano
Gatto
Genovese
Giacobelli
Giacopetti
Gianolo
Giovannelli

Giovannetti
Lo Bianco
Lo Verde
Luna
Mancini
Mancuso
Messina
Morelli
Morena
Napoli
Oliva
Pisciolo
Ragazzi

Ragazzo
Ricci
Rizzo
Rossi
Santangelo
Scarpello
Serrano
Sorrentino
Testa
Tonelli
Volpe

Given Names

Male:

Adriano
Aldo
Alessandro
Amerigo
Anastagio
Angelo
Antonio
Arnaldo
Arturo
Baldassare
Benedetto
Bruno
Cesare
Cristoforo
Dominico
Donatello
Donato
Edoardo
Enrico
Enzo
Ernesto

Fabio
Fausto
Federico
Flavio
Giacommo
Giamo
Giancarlo
Gilberto
Gino
Giorgio
Giovanni
Giulio
Giuseppe
Giustino
Gregorio
Guido
Guiseppi
Gustavo
Ignazio
Lazzaro
Leonardo

Lorenzo
Luciano
Luigi
Marcello
Marco
Mario
Martino
Nuncio
Paolo
Rafaele
Renzo
Roberto
Romano
Salvatore
Sebastiano
Sergio
Silvano
Stefano
Uberto
Vito
Vittorio

Female:

Agnella	Elisabetta	Nicia
Agnese	Emma	Olimpia
Angela	Fabiana	Philippa
Anna	Fiorenza	Pia
Anna Maria	Flavia	Rachele
Belinda	Francesca	Regina
Bianca	Gabriela	Rosa
Brigida	Giacinta	Rosalia
Bruna	Gianina	Rosamaria
Candida	Gina	Sabrina
Cara	Giovanna	Sancia
Carita	Irene	Sofia
Carmelina	Isabella	Teresa
Catarina	Leona	Tonia
Cecilia	Lia	Trista
Cella	Luisa	Valentina
Constantina	Manuela	Violetta
Cristina	Maria	

SCANDINAVIAN

Surnames

Anderson	Hedstrom	Lundgren
Andreasson	Heg	Nilsson
Bjornstad	Holm	Olsson
Blegen	Jansson	Peterson
Bremer	Johansson	Strand
Carlsson	Karlsson	Strom
Dahl	Larsen	Svenson
Eriksson	Lind	Swenson

(Surnames ending in "son" are most often Swedish, those ending in "sen" are usually Norwegian or Danish.)

Given Names

Male:

Alf	Gregor	Magnus
Alrik	Gunnar	Martin
Amund	Gustav	Mats
Anders	Hans	Max
Anton	Hansel	Morten
Arens	Henrik	Nels
Arne	Hugo	Nils
Arvid	Igor	Olaf
Axell	Ingeborg	Ole
Bengt	Ingmar	Pal
Bertil	Jan	Per
Bjorn	Jens	Poul
Borg	Johan	Roald
Dag	Jon	Sigurd
Dana	Jorgen	Skipp
Davin	Josef	Soren
Dreng	Kalle	Stian
Elvis	Karl	Sutherland
Erik	Kjell	Sven
Evan	Knute	Thomas
Frans	Konrad	Tor
Fredrik	Lars	Ulf
Garth	Leif	

Female:

Agneta	Brenda	Dorte
Anete	Brigitta	Edit
Anna	Brit	Eldrid
Anne	Brita	Elise
Annika	Camilla	Else
Arla	Cathrine	Erica
Astrid	Charlotta	Eva
Aud	Dagmar	Frida
Audhild	Dagny	Gala
Barbro	Disa	Gerda
Birgit	Dorotea	Gressa

Greta	Jomina	Meri
Gudrun	Jorunn	Mona
Gunda	Karen	Nina
Gunilla	Katarina	Ola
Hanne	Katrina	Olga
Harriet	Kelsey	Rakel
Hedda	Kerstin	Rona
Helga	Kristin	Sigrid
Hilde	Kristine	Silje
Hildegunn	Lotta	Sonja
Ida	Magna	Trine
Inga	Maj	Trude
Ingeborg	Marianne	Ulla
Ingemar	Marja	Vera
Ingrid	Marta	Yvonne

RUSSIAN

Surnames

Alekseyevna	Kocyk	Popov
Alexandrova	Kolodenko	Seriyev
Andreev	Kosloff	Skirski
Belofsky	Malenkov	Skulsky
Bocharova	Maranovich	Sokolov
Burgasov	Mikhailov	Stepovich
Fedorov	Minsky	Tomich
Fedulova	Nenasheva	Vasilev
Gromeko	Nikiforov	Yakovlev
Horwitz	Orloff	Zlotnikov
Ivanov	Petrov	Zosimoff
Ivanovich	Petrovich	

Given Names

Male:

Alexander	Anatolii	Aronoff
Alexei	Andrey	Artur
Alik	Anton	Boris

Burian	Karlov	Pasha
Cheslav	Karol	Pavel
Danya	Klim	Petrov
Denis	Kolya	Pyotr
Dima	Konstantin	Rodia
Dimitry	Kostoff	Roman
Egor	Kubik	Sergei
Evgenii	Leonid	Stanislav
Fabiyan	Lev	Stanko
Fedor	Levka	Stas
Filip	Matkovich	Stephan
Fredek	Matvey	Tomas
Fyodor	Michael	Valerii
Garald	Mikhail	Vassily
Georgii	Mishkin	Victor
Gorya	Motka	Vladimir
Grigori	Nicodemus	Yakov
Igor	Nikolai	Yuri
Ivan	Oleg	Ziv

Female:

Alena	Ekaterina	Lesya
Alexandr	Elena	Lina
Alina	Evgenia	Ludmila
Alla	Feodora	Magda
Alma	Galina	Mara
Alya	Gayla	Marina
Anastasia	Inessa	Marinka
Anna	Irina	Nadia
Antonina	Ivana	Nastasia
Anya	Katerina	Nastia
Asia	Katya	Nessa
Bruna	Kira	Nika
Dasha	Kisa	Olena
Dina	Kiska	Olesya
Dominika	Lara	Olga
Dounia	Larisa	Olyona
Duscha	Lenora	Panya

Pasha
Sabina
Sacha
Sasha
Sashenka
Sonya

Svetlana
Tanya
Tasya
Tatyana
Tonya
Ursula

Valentina
Vanya
Varenka
Vera
Vilma
Zoya

ARABIC

Surnames

Abdo
Abdoo
Ali
Aziz
Fuad
Habib
Haddad
Hakim
Hammad
Hassan

Hassar
Hassim
Ibrahim
Igbal
Khalil
Khalof
Khoury
Mahdi
Mallah
Maloof

Mura
Mustafa
Naggar
Najib
Shadid
Sharif
Suleiman
Yahya
Yusuf

Given Names

Male: (Male names are frequently prefixed with Abdul, Abdel Abd or Ibn.)

Abda
Abdel
Adib
Afdal
Ahmad
Ahsan
Akram
Ashraf
Bahar
Basam
Boutros
Dahab
Djmal

Fadoul
Faisal
Farukh
Fawzy
Habib
Hafiz
Haj
Hashim
Izzat
Kamal
Karim
Madjid
Musa

Nadim
Nassar
Quamar
Rafi
Rashid
Saffa
Wassif
Yasir

Female:

Abida	Hayfa	Radheeda
Adiva	Hinda	Raisa
Almira	Jahara	Saarah
Amineh	Jamila	Sabira
Ayasha	Kabira	Safia
Baraka	Karida	Shereen
Basima	Leyla	Tamarat
Dahab	Malika	Wajida
Fadiyla	Marid	Zafina
Fatma	Nadira	Zarifa
Habideh	Najia	Zohar
Hajar	Qadira	

JAPANESE

Surnames

Arita	Iwata	Okawara
Endo	Kawa	Okudara
Fuji	Kikumura	Shibayaku
Fujita	Kobayashi	Suzuki
Fujiyama	Kume	Tagawa
Fukuyama	Kuroda	Takahashi
Furuta	Matsu	Takayama
Hakata	Matsumoto	Tanabe
Hirata	Mizuochi	Tanaka
Hoshi	Morita	Uchiyama
Inoue	Moto	Yamada
Ishiguro	Nakagawa	Yamamoto
Iwamoto	Nakamura	Yanagiya
Iwasaki	Noda	Yawashita

Given Names

Male:

Akio	Hiroshi	Jo
Akira	Hisoka	Joji
Hiroki	Ichi	Jun
Hiromasa	Jiro	Junzo

Kazuhiro	Naoko	Taro
Ken	Saburo	Tomi
Kin	Samuru	Tomosuki
Kyoshi	Satoshi	Toshio
Kasahiro	Shiro	Yasuo
Misao	Takeshi	Yukio

Female:

Ai	Hiroko	Mitsu
Aiko	Hisaka	Miyoko
Aki	Hoshi	Moto
Arasuki	Hoshiko	Nami
Asa	Ima	Nyoko
Ayame	Ishi	Rai
Azami	Jin	Raku
Chika	Jun	Reiko
Chikako	Kaiyo	Sachi
Chiyo	Kata	Sachiko
Chizu	Kawa	Sakura
Cho	Kiku	Sato
Dai	Kin	Setzu
Etsu	Koto	Shizu
Gen	Kuri	Suki
Gin	Kyoko	Suzu
Hama	Kyoshi	Taka
Hanako	Mai	Toshi
Harulu	Matsu	Umeko
Hatsu	Midori	Yoko
Hideyo	Miki	Yoshiko

CHINESE

Surnames

Chan	Eng	Kwan
Chang	Fu	Lee
Chew	Han	Li
Chou	Ho	Liao
Chow	Hung	Ling

Ming	Teng	Won
Ng	Toy	Wu
Song	Wang	Xu
Soo	Wing	

Given Names

Male:

An	Hung	Quon
Anguo	Jin	Shen
Chen	Jun	Shilin
Chi	Keung	Shoi-ming
Chung	Li	Sying
Deshi	Liang	Tsun-chung
Dewei	Liko	Tung
Dingbang	Lok	Wang
Gan	Manchu	Wing
Ho	Ming-hoa	Zhiyuan
Hop	On	
Huang Fu	Park	

Female:

Ah Cy	Fung	Mei
Ah Lam	Guan-yin	Meizhen
Bik	Hu	Ming-hua
Bo	Hua	Sya
Chao-xing	Hwei-ru	Tao
Chow	Jun	Te
Chu-hua	Lee	Yet Kwai
Chun	Lian	Yow
Chyou	Lien-hua	Yuet
Da Chun	Li-hua	Yuke
Eu-meh	Lin	
Far	Ling	

7
Character Homes

adobe: a clay and straw brick house, common in the American Southwest.

A-frame: a small, vacation home, shaped like a triangle or the letter *A*.

bothy: a small English or Scottish cottage.

brownstone: any home or apartment building faced with reddish brown sandstone.

bungalow: a cottage-like home, usually having one or one-and-a-half stories, with overhanging gables.

cajun cottage: slang term for a tin-roofed shack found in Louisiana.

Cape Cod: a one-and-half story house with a sharply pitched roof, originating in Cape Cod, Massachusetts, and common throughout New England.

carpenter gothic: any nineteenth-century home incorporating decorative gothic motifs.

catslide house: slang term for a saltbox.

chateau: a French country estate.

colonial: a broad term encompassing a number of house styles adopted from Europe, but commonly designating a two-story, rectangular house with a pitched roof.

Creole townhouse: the classic New Orleans townhouse, with stuccoed facades in pink, ochre and yellow; iron balconies; slate or tiled roofs; and arched and shuttered windows.

dacha: a Russian cottage or vacation house.

duplex: a house divided in half for two separate sets of tenants.

Dutch colonial: a two-story, rectangular house having a roof with two different pitches per side.

Elizabethan: an English design of the 1500s, identified by its large, mullioned windows and decorative strapwork.

Federal: originating in the period from 1790 to 1830 and since revived, a classic design characterized by round or oval rooms, two (and sometimes four) chimneys flanking either end of the roof, twin front stairways, brass and iron hardware, and elaborate fan doorways.

flat: an apartment with only one floor.

gambrel: See Dutch colonial.

garrison: a two-story colonial with a slightly overhanging second floor.

Georgian: a two-story colonial characterized by a columned or pilaster-flanked front entry, heavy stone sills, brass hardware and ornate roof balustrades.

gingerbread house: any ornately designed house of the nineteenth century reminiscent of the fairy tale house.

Greek Revival: a classic, Greek- and Roman-inspired home with a temple-like facade comprised of Corinthian, Doric or Ionic wood-columned portico and foliate-carved door surrounds and eves, originating in the early nineteenth century.

hacienda: a large Spanish estate.

houseboat: a barge-like boat designed for year-round living.

Italianate: a style popular in the United States and in England in the mid 1800s, an Italian villa-like house with slightly pitched roofs, square towers and round-arched windows.

log cabin: a rustic home constructed of rough-hewn logs.

mansion: any large, opulent home.

mobile home: an inexpensive, prefab, one-story home that can be transported to one's own private site or to a mobile home park.

octagon: an eight-sided house of the Victorian era.

penthouse: an apartment or condominium set on the roof of a building.

prefab: any bland, Monopoly-board house prefabricated in a factory.

pueblo: a stone or adobe community house, sometimes as high as five stories, of the southwestern United States.

Queen Anne: a popular design of the 1870s and 1880s and widely revived in the 1970s, 1980s and 1990s, a house combining Elizabethan, Tudor, Gothic and English Renaissance forms, with polygonal or cylindrical towers, bay windows, balconies, and richly decorated woodwork.

ranch: an American one-story house, sometimes elongated.

row house: any house in a long line of matching houses.

saltbox: a box-like house with a long, sharply pitched roof in back and a short-pitched roof in front, popular in New England.

Second Empire: a Victorian era house with mansard roofs, high arched windows and doors, and iron roof pinnacles.

shanty: a shack.

tenement: a low-rent, multi-unit apartment building, usually found in the run-down parts of a city.

town house: a two- or three-story house joined to other similar houses in the city.

trailer: any recreational vehicle made into a permanent home.

Tudor: a house style characterized by its large, exposed beams.